T0381440

VEEJACK

The Stealth Religion Destroying Judeo-Christian America

ROBERT F. STAMPS

WESTBOW
PRESS®
A DIVISION OF THOMAS NELSON
& ZONDERVAN

WestBow Press books may be ordered through booksellers or by contacting:

WestBow Press
A Division of Thomas Nelson & Zondervan
1663 Liberty Drive
Bloomington, IN 47403
www.westbowpress.com
844-714-3454

A.B., with Distinction in Political Science, University of Illinois
J.D., Wake Forest University
LL.M, International and Comparative Law, George Washington University
M.A., Theology, Loyola Marymount University – Theta Alpha Kappa Honor Society

Las Vegas: Ascension Enterprises

ISBN: 979-8-3850-3181-8 (sc)
ISBN: 979-8-3850-3182-5 (e)

Library of Congress Control Number: 2024916934

Print information available on the last page.

WestBow Press rev. date: 08/26/2024

Veejack†

"The hearing ear and the seeing eye – the Lord
has made them both" – Proverbs 20:12

"Let Anyone with Ears Listen!" – Matthew 11:15

"Though seeing, they do not see;
though hearing, they do not hear or
understand" – Matthew 13:13

† Values Inconsistent with Judaic and Christian Theology
(VIWJCT – Pronounced Veejack)™

CONTENTS

Introduction   ix

Foreword   xiii

1. The Beginnings and Formations of Religions   1

2. First Amendment Guarantees and Protections   20

3. Marx and Engels Originate the VeeJack Religion   31

4. The Veejack Religion and Why it Refuses to Identify Itself   45

5. Generating Mass Movements and Discord   65

6. Veejack Religious Practices and Values   80

7. Climate and the Weather Gods   84

8. Veejack Religion Invents Lawfare   110

9. Syncretic Judeo-Christian Camouflage   123

Bibliography   131

CONTENTS

Introduction

1. The 10

2. The Nature of .... Duration

3. ...... Insights .... Back End

4. The .... and Why ......

5. .... Math ....

6. ......

7. ...... and the ......

8. ...... Release 110

9. ......

Bibliography

INTRODUCTION

The inspiration for this manuscript occurred while writing the thesis for my master's in theology. My thesis is entitled "The Phenomenon of the Nones – And Faith in the Holy Spirit" and it discusses disaffiliation from Christian denominations. The title uses the colloquial term "Nones", describing the people who check "None of the Above" on religious affiliation surveys.

The reasons that Nones provide to researchers for leaving their churches include the prohibition of women from leadership roles in many denominations, rejection of the LGBTQ community, clerical abuse of children, and opposition to abortion. Others just drift away from their churches because they are busy doing other things. My view is that God's love is not androcentric, extends to all people, and the church must recognize and act on its responsibilities and be accountable for wrongdoing perpetrated in its name or by its leaders.

As my research into the Nones progressed, I began to recognize that in addition to the internal reasons for disaffiliation, there is an external, often unrecognized force pulling people away. And the external force was broader than expected as it impacts all Judeo-Christian faith. For the past forty years the Judeo-Christian faith has suffered a relentless assault by the news reporters in electronic and print media, talk show participants, politicians, academics and educational administrators, social media influencers, and performing artists. The assault targets Judeo-Christian faiths by focusing on the negative, inflammatory, and predatory behaviors and activities of a minority of individuals in leadership positions. These incidents are widely circulated by the anti-Judeo-Christian forces in attempts to demean the faiths and influence people to believe the whole Judeo-Christian model is corrupt and should be abolished.

Realization that there is an external force targeting and tarnishing the Judeo-Christian faiths fostered a secondary realization. The external force attempting to destroy Judeo-Christian faiths is actually a competing religion; a competing, nontheistic, often hedonistic and self-destructive religion that dares not publicly announce its existence.

The proponents of the new religion purposely ignore the vastly more numerous and significantly beneficial Judeo-Christian activities that occur every day across the United States. Judeo-Christian activities such as molding moral behavior in youths; educating oppressed and impoverished people; providing free food, shelter, and health care to the indigent; providing counseling; visiting the sick, infirm and elderly and those in hospice care; assisting addicts to regain their freedom by helping them to eliminate dependence on addictive substances; and calming gang violence. These, and a host of other unheralded and unreported positive Judeo-Christian activities are ignored by the propagandists of the new religion.

The new religion and its media influencers portray the Judeo-Christian faiths in the worst light possible. The new religion's politicians legislate its religious beliefs into law. The new religion's clerics, functioning as journalists, or researchers, or academics, or broadcast personalities paint a slanted, negative, one-sided portrait of Judeo-Christian faiths and praise the tenets of the new religion.

If the media, influencers, and pop culture focused on the unsung heroes of the Judeo-Christian faiths who toil day in and day out to live God's message of love and joy the faiths would not be the subject of invective, abuse, and diminished membership. It is unrealistic, however, for the Judeo-Christian faiths to expect the followers of the new religion to change their views and portray Judeo-Christian faiths honestly and in a more positive light. Instead, the new faith must be identified and subjected to the same legal parameters as other religions. The purpose of this manuscript is to identify the parameters of the new religion and illuminate its beliefs, practices, and activities.

FOREWORD

The colonies that formed the United States of America were founded by immigrants seeking a place to practice their religion and protect themselves from persecution for their religious beliefs. The formation of the United States was a bold experiment, unique in the history of the world, in which the people would govern themselves and – most importantly – protect the right of all people to practice the religion of their choice. Freedom of religion was so important to the new nation that it enshrined the doctrine of freedom of religion, and the equally important prohibition that the government must never engage in religion, in the First Amendment to the United States Constitution.[1]

The First Amendment states that "Congress shall make no law respecting an establishment of religion, or prohibiting the free exercise thereof . . ."[2] In these few words the framers provided two entitlements to the people. The first and most important entitlement is a prohibition that the government may not establish a religion. The second entitlement is the right of all people to practice the religion of their choice.

The legal regime for protection of religion in the United States evolved as the nation grew. Protections for religious practice grew as immigration increased from countries that did not practice

---

[1] U.S. Const, Amend 1. See, infra, Chapter 2, "First Amendment Guarantees and Protections".

[2] *Ibid.*

religion in the Abrahamic traditions.[3] For instance, immigration was originally from religions in the Judeo-Christian traditions.[4] However, as immigration brought Islamic, Hindu, Buddhist, and other faiths into the United States the First Amendment protected them, and also protected the religious practices of the indigenous Native Americans.

The prohibition against the government engaging in religion also evolved and expanded to include prohibiting the individual state governments from establishing a religion.[5] Religious practices such as the worship of God, the reverence for and worship of Jesus, the veneration of Saints, readings from the Bible and telling of Biblical stories, and prayer were supported and opposed in the courts and legislatures.

Now, however, for the first time in the history of the United States the people are faced with a new problem: the government is actively engaged in the establishment of an official religion – a stealth religion that refuses to acknowledge itself and cloaks its fanaticism in political rhetoric. Unfortunately, either purposely or inadvertently government policy makers at the Federal, state, and local levels have let the new religion capture many of the powers of government through the simple ruse of its failing to identify itself as a religion. Instead, the new stealth religion presents its beliefs, practices, vocabulary, and actions as "truth" that is required by equity and/or diversity or is necessary to rectify previous exclusions or discrimination. The stealth religion identifies its adherents as

---

[3] The Abrahamic religions include Judaism, Christianity, and Islam. Abraham is mentioned in Genesis 17-18 and Quaran 2:124 and 16:120.

[4] Going forward when the interests of the Judaic and Christian religions are similar, they will be identified as "Judeo-Christian".

[5] U.S. Const, Amend 14. This Amendment reads, in part, "nor shall any state deprive any person of life, liberty, or property, without due process of law; . ." The United States Supreme Court ruled that the 14th Amendment incorporates almost all of the Bill of Rights (i.e., Amendments 1 through 10). See, e.g., *Everson v. Board of Education*, 330 U.S. 1 (1947).

victims of persecution, either by the government or by Judeo-Christian peoples or both.

Nothing could be further from the truth. Wrapping itself in pious rhetoric, the stealth religion professes that its doctrines are "truth" that is unshackled to religion. It is an error to view the passion of its supporters as dispositive when they speak their views as "truth." Instead, there needs to be rigorous enforcement of the First Amendment's prohibition on the establishment of a state-supported religion. It is an error to view the passion of its supporters as supporting that their spiritual views are equitable and not religious as a justification for funneling taxpayer money to new and unproven technologies demanded by and manufactured by its elites. It is an error to view the passion of its supporters[6] as a justification for proselytizing its views as "education" in the public schools or to justify its attacks within the public schools on Judeo-Christian theological beliefs.

Because the new stealth religion fails to identify itself by name it will be known, for the purpose of this discussion, as a religion advocating Values Inconsistent with Judaic and Christian Theology (VIWJCT). Since this phrase is overly long, and the acronym VIWJCT is not susceptible to ready pronunciation, it will be written and pronounced "Veejack" as a means to identify the new stealth religion.[7]

The Veejack religion's stealth characteristics, existence and

---

[6] Many of the stealth religion's supporters do not know that they have been converted and imagine they adhere to a different religion (e.g., Judaism, Catholicism, Protestantism, Hinduism, Islam, etc.).

[7] Other commentators have come close to recognizing Veejack as a religion using nouns such as "socialism", "woke", and "progressive". The use of such nouns, which have preexisting and/or alternate meanings, has allowed the practitioners of the Veejack religion to quibble with the commentators and peddle arguments about the precise meaning of these nouns. Instead, the term Veejack is unique and has not previously been used. Unless and until the practitioners of the religion of Veejack come forth and identify themselves with their own name, the term Veejack must suffice. For brevity in these Notes, the term "Veejack" will be used to identify the Veejack religion.

socialist underpinnings are affirmed by an observation of philosopher Ernest Renan. Renan wrote that, "religion is not a popular error; it is a great instinctive truth, sensed by the people, expressed by the people."[8] And Eric Hoffer observed that Renan's insight " . . . was that socialism was the coming religion of the Occident, and that being a secular religion it would lead to a (religion) of politics and economics."[9] Hoffer's profound insight that belief in the doctrines of socialism lead inevitably to a religion of politics and economics is faulty only in that the religion that has now established itself within the governments of the United States is not secular – the new religion of politics and economics is a religion, albeit the new religion is nontheistic.

George Orwell also perceptively predicted the Veejack religion's elites' efforts to mold society into their vision of utopia – in which they, the Veejack religion's elites, would rule and the people would do their bidding. The Veejack religion's vision of rising to power is mockingly depicted in Orwell's dystopian novel of suffering and injustice *Animal Farm*.[10] This novel depicts a fictional British farm on which the animals revolt and displace the human farm workers. The reasoning put forth by the pigs, who rule the other animals, is that they must remove humans "from the scene, and (then) the root cause of hunger and overwork is abolished forever."[11]

The pigs decided they must accomplish the "work of teaching and organizing the others . . . (because the pigs) were generally recognized as being the cleverest of the animals."[12] Unlike the Veejack religion, which cloaks itself in invisibility, the pigs gave a name to their ideology: "Animalism".[13] The pigs mock the rival theology of "Sugarcandy Mountain"; a faith that promised all animals went to

[8] https://libquotes.com/ernest-renan/quote/lbr9i4x
[9] Hoffer, Eric, The True Believer – Thoughts on the Nature of Mass Movements, New York: Harper Perennial Modern Classics, 2010, at 158.
[10] Orwell, George, *Animal Farm*, Istanbul/Turkiye: Oteki Adam, 2023.
[11] Orwell, *Animal Farm*, 6.
[12] Orwell, *Animal Farm*, 11.
[13] Orwell, *Animal Farm*, 11.

Sugarcandy Mountain when they died; which is clearly Orwell's substitute for Judeo-Christian beliefs.[14] As many of the farm animals believed in Sugarcandy Mountain, "the pigs had to argue very hard to persuade them that there was no such place."[15]

As with the Veejack religion's elites, "(t)he pigs did not actually work, but directed and supervised the others. With their superior knowledge it was natural that they should assume the leadership."[16] And, "(i)t had come to be accepted that the pigs, who were manifestly cleverer than the other animals, should decide all questions of . . . policy . . .."[17] As food supplies dwindled, the pigs found it necessary to mold language – a trait adopted by the Veejack religion – and so food rations never had a "reduction"; instead when food supplies decreased they were announced as a "readjustment."[18] Finally, the pigs adopted more and more human traits. And Orwell's famous line, repeated often in reference to the Veejack religion's elites as they claim special privileges, comes from this novel. Orwell wrote of the pigs' right to have better living conditions and more food, and better living arrangements over the other animals because, even though "all animals are equal . . . some animals are more equal than others."[19]

As the other animals observed the pigs interacting and drinking alcohol with humans the animals outside looked from pig to human, and from human to pig, but ". . . it was impossible to say which was which."[20] This is true with the Veejack religion's theology as it portrays itself as protecting people while actually subjugating them to harsher conditions than existed before. This is evident in the Veejack religion's cities such as New York, Chicago, San Francisco and other areas where crime, corruption, wanton psychotic behavior,

---

[14] Orwell, *Animal Farm*, 12.
[15] Orwell, *Animal Farm*, 12.
[16] Orwell, *Animal Farm*, 18.
[17] Orwell, *Animal Farm*, 31.
[18] Orwell, *Animal Farm*, 70.
[19] Orwell, *Animal Farm*, 84
[20] Orwell, *Animal Farm*, 88.

homelessness, high food prices, and other detriments to pleasant living abound.

The Veejack religion has every right to exist, propagate its views and faith, and discipline its members. However, it has no right to independence from the Constitutional constraints on establishing a state religion. And its hostility to existing religions and non-religious people must be curbed. As will be discussed later, the new religion has adopted literature that warned against fanaticism, totalitarianism, and state religion as guides for establishing their religion as a state religion. The new religion has upended the perceptive insights and warnings about the horrors of totalitarian fanaticism from social philosophers like Eric Hoffer and Geoge Orwell. The Veejack religion has turned Hoffer's and Orwell's warnings about fascism into "how to" manuals to spread their religion. It uses the warnings of the societal agonies depicted in Orwell's dystopian science fiction novel as a guide to implement and forge its own authoritarian movement. With Orwell's cautions about fascism as guidelines and aided by Hoffer's spectacular analysis of previous fascistic movements, the Veejack religion is writing the blueprint for its religious beliefs and at the same time it is imposing its political agenda on society.

The Veejack religious faith is actively hostile to, opposed to, and vociferously critical of the Jewish and Christian faiths.[21] The new religion strongly opposes Judeo-Christian values, rejects the Ten Commandments, mirrors Canaanite and other primitive religious practices, and encourages hedonism and other self-destructive behaviors in the guise of self-sacrifice.[22] The Veejack religion's

---

[21] Philosopher and author Ernest Renan wrote that "It is through Christianity that Judaism has really conquered the world. Christianity is the masterpiece of Judaism." See, e.g., Renan, Ernest, "History of the People of Israel – Till the Time of King David", London: Chapman and Hall, Ltd., 1888; and Renan, Ernest, "The History of the Origins of Christianity, London: Mathieson & Co., 1863-1890.

[22] Even geographic maps reflect the prejudice against the Judeo-Christian faiths as reflected in Kornick, Lindsay, "Brooklyn classroom displays Qatar-funded map where Israel is replaced with Palestine: report", January 12, 2024 at https://www.foxnews.com/media/brooklyn-classroom-displays-qatar-funded-map-where-israel-replaced-

values and beliefs are inconsistent with Judeo-Christian ethics and teachings. The Veejack religion openly encourages violence, and uses Constitutional freedoms to petition the government, attend governmental meetings, and demonstrate in public places as steppingstones to violent confrontation. The Veejack religion has no moral code and rejects the concept of "sin" itself.[23]

The Veejack religion within the United States argues that the United States has never been "perfect." The Veejack religion incorporates politics and economics and teaches that the United States, and the European colonies that formed or merged with the United States, sanctioned morally repugnant behaviors. The morally repugnant practices within the United States, acknowledged widely beyond the Veejack religion, included slavery, racial and religious bigotry, gender discrimination, sexual orientation discrimination, wrongful incarcerations, and other discrimination based on *inter alia* color, ethnicity, creed, age, class, sexual identify, and mental and/or physical ability.[24]

The Veejack religion does not recognize that the United States is leading the world in eradicating discrimination. Instead, the Veejack religion believes the Federal and state governments must be toppled as punishment for their forebears' sins; and replaced by a new utopia run by the economic, academic, and social elites. Pending

---

palestine-report. The report states that a school in Brooklyn, NY has a map with Israel replaced by the name "Palestine."

[23] Hoffer, at 54, reflects on "what a task confronts the American clergy . . . preaching the good news of a Savior to people who for the most part have no real sense of sin."

[24] The views of the new religion opposing gender discrimination and sexual orientation are not unique. Other religions share these views. However, various Judeo-Christian sects – including the Roman Catholic church – do not share this belief. For example, the teaching of the Roman Catholic church does not support gender ideology. See, e.g., Zengarini, Lisa, "Pope Francis: Gender ideology is the ugliest danger of our time," Vatican News at https://www.vaticannews.va/en/pope/news/2024-03/pope-francis-gender-ideology-is-the-ugliest-danger-of-our-time.html. See, also, *Declaration of the Dicastery for the Doctrine of the Faith "Dignitas Infinita" on Human Dignity, 08.04.2024* at https://press.vatican.va/content/salastampa/en/bollettino/pubblico/2024/04/08/240408c.html.

the destruction of the United States, the Veejack religion's elites maintain themselves in comfort so that when the bad governments fall, they – the elites – will be rested and ready so they may assume the roles of leadership and punish the wrongdoers who ruled the previously oppressive society.

The VeeJack religion's values and teachings challenge, are opposed to, and even mock, the Judeo-Christian faiths. The Veejack religion vigorously challenges Judeo-Christian religious beliefs in public education and government. But its leaders disrespect the mandate of the Constitution and the United States' tradition of keeping religion out of government when it comes to its own Veejack religious beliefs.

The Veejack religion may, and probably does, exist outside the United States, but this analysis is limited to the Veejack religion within the United States. Individual Veejack religious adherents will not be identified as many of them would argue that they adhere to a different religious belief. It is the Veejack religion's beliefs, not its adherents, which must be barred from public education, legislative initiatives, and executive action. Many of the Veejack religion's beliefs will be identified herein, but other Veejack religious beliefs must in the future be identified by Judeo-Christian, Islamic, and other theological scholars.[25] As the Veejack religion's beliefs that have insinuated themselves into government are identified they must be

---

[25] Scholars of Islam's rich cultural, intellectual, and theological beliefs and traditions are encouraged to delve into Veejack's dogmas and uncover and expose those which conflict with the tenets of Islam and yet are still taught in the public schools. Islamic youths in public education, like their Jewish and Christian colleagues are being indoctrinated into the Veejack religion, a religion that is antithetical to their Islamic faith. As Wikipedia's entry on the Quran (also Koran) explains, "the Quran was revealed by God to the final Islamic prophet Muhammad through the angel Gabriel incrementally over a period of some 23 years, beginning on the Night of Power, when Muhammad was 40, and concluding in 632, the year of his death. Muslims regard the Quran as Muhammad's most important miracle, a proof of his prophethood, and the culmination of a series of divine messages starting with those revealed to the first Islamic prophet Adam, including the Islamic holy books of the Torah, Psalms, and Gospel." See, https://en.wikipedia.org/wiki/Quran

recognized as religious beliefs and excluded from public education and legislative funding.

While the Veejack religion fails to identify itself as a religion with a name, it does advance its doctrines as devotion to "truth". It constantly opposes Judeo-Christian beliefs and practices and passes itself off as embodying modern feelings, beliefs, and societal norms. The new religion is characterized by beliefs[26] that are not an ideology, but are instead a nascent, non-theistic religious movement.[27] It is modernistic in that it does not utilize a house of worship such as a church, synagogue, mosque, temple, or even an in-home alter. Instead, its adherents use non-traditional worship spaces such as social media, broadcast media on television and radio, or the internet. Its pulpit is often the airwaves, with informal elastic messaging on radio or television, internet messaging applications, or streaming services. Socialist cable broadcast influencers have even referred to their "sacred airwaves."[28] The Veejack religion's texts are unique as well, often being found on informational websites.

---

[26] The terminology of this new religion, as with the religion itself, is cloaked and concealed behind terms that have indeterminate meaning. The most common terms include woke, socialist, and DEI (i.e., diversity, equity, inclusion). Although these terms are widely used, they have no common definition or accepted meaning. Initially, the terms were used to evoke a condescending attitude of superiority. For example, a "woke" person was described as aware of, and concerned about, social injustice, societal inequality, and espoused socialistic views. Soon, however, the term "woke" became an epithet aimed at supercilious left-leaning media pundits, academics, and politicians. Use of the term "woke" provokes disagreement as to its meaning, so it will not be used in this monograph unless as an attributable direct quote. Similarly, the term "socialist" is generally rejected because of its connection to NAZIs (National Socialism), Communists (e.g., Union of Soviet Socialist Republics), Fascists (policies rooted in national socialism) and other ideologies denounced in the United States; although many of Veejack's beliefs, tactics, and doctrines are reflective of these earlier quasi-religious movements.

[27] As will be discussed, *infra*, religions need not be theistic, or recognize a deity.

[28] See, e.g., Wulfsohn, Joseph A., "NBC's Ronna McDaniel meltdown: Falsehoods and debunked narratives MSNBC promoted on its 'sacred airwaves'", March 30, 2024 at https://www.foxnews.com/media/nbcs-ronna-mcdaniel-meltdown-falsehoods-debunked-narratives-msnbc-promoted-sacred-airwaves, quoting MSNBC host Nicolle Wallace.

Interestingly, the Veejack religion has many superficial similarities to the Eastern religions of Buddhism and Hinduism, and to primitive religions that arose on all the settled continents in pre-historic times.

The Veejack religion and its practitioners do not publicly admit their adherence to the stealth religion. They do not self-identify as a religion, or even admit their reality as a genuine religious faith. The Veejack religion's leadership recognizes that once it admits its existence as a religion it will lose its ability to control public schools, legislative funding, and other aspects of government. Therefore, a religious researcher, instead of attending the Veejack religion's spiritual services or interviewing the Veejack religion's leaders, must obtain an intellectual and religious understanding of the Veejack religion by observation, analysis, and common sense.

This monograph is an attempt to define the outer parameters of the Veejack religion so that political leaders, theologians, academics, jurists, and especially ordinary people may comprehend that the new "truths" being espoused by the Veejack religion are not "truths" at all – they are only "truths" for the Veejack religion's believers. For comparison, many religions existed for hundreds of years without being recognized as distinct religions. The Veejack religion is at same stage of development as when Constantine recognized Christianity in the Roman Empire in the early 4th century CE; when Mohammed moved from Mecca to Medina (622 CE); and when Siddhartha Gautama's (Buddha's) nontheistic teachings began to spread in South Asia in the 6th or 5th century BCE.[29] Another interesting parallel to now identifying the Veejack religion as a religion is the intellectual observation of 16th century Dutch jurist and scholar, Hugo Grotius, who recognized the existence of, and identified the tenets of the genus

---

[29] Please note that Veejack's anti-Christian passion has been successful in eliminating the historically traditional dating mechanisms of B.C., meaning Before Christ, and A.D., meaning *Anno Domini*, which translates as "in the year of our Lord". The new dating nomenclature, imposed by Veejack's academic adherents, are BCE, meaning "Before the Common Era," and CE, meaning "Common Era". For consistency with current practice, the Veejack forms of BCE and CE will be used to signify historical dates.

of international law.[30] Grotius accomplished this by recognizing the system of principles that were then internationally held binding on all people and nations. By recognizing that international law existed, Grotius changed the course of history. Hopefully, recognition of the Veejack faith as a religion will place it on an equal plane with the Judeo-Christian, Islamic, Buddhist, Hindu and other recognized religious faiths and make its beliefs subject to the First Amendment.

The Veejack religion is vehemently opposed to Judeo-Christian values, practices, and symbols. The Veejack religion's believers are taught to be repulsed by images of the Star of David, manger scenes, the cross, the crucifixion and crucifixes, and Judeo-Christian statuary and buildings. The Veejack religion's adherents are taught to mock these symbols and even vandalize them.[31] The Veejack religion's opposition to Judeo-Christian teachings, beliefs, practices, history, symbols, holidays, and a host of other negative and opprobrious actions against the Judeo-Christian faiths should be enough to ban the Veejack religion's teachings from the public schools and prohibit the use of government funds for its messages. However, it is not merely the Veejack religion's antipathy to Judeo-Christian faiths that require judicial officers enforcing the Constitution to cast it out of the governmental orb. It is that the Veejack religion has identifiable and sustained religious beliefs, functions, and symbology. The Veejack religion is a nontheistic, semi-primitive belief system that must not be publicly funded or taught.

---

[30] Britannica at https://www.britannica.com/biography/Hugo-Grotius. Grotius (April 10, 1583 to August 28, 1645), wrote *De Jure Belli ac Pacis* and is considered the "father of international law."

[31] See, e.g., Tietz, Kendall, "Religious-themed designs banned from White House Easter egg art contest," March 29, 2024, at https://www.foxnews.com/media/religious-themed-designs-banned-white-house-easter-egg-art-contest, in which President Joseph Biden does not present the Christian holiday celebrating Christ's resurrection as a religious celebration. Instead, Easter is mocked and caricatured as a hunt for eggs; and any reference to religion is specifically prohibited. See, also, Nelson, Joseph Q., "Washington teacher says schools must do more to keep students' info secret from 'Christo-fascist' parents," February 25, 2023. At https://www.foxnews.com/media/washington-teacher-says-schools-keep-students-info-secret-christo-fascist-parents.

The practice of Veejackianism is a religious faith, and its beliefs must remain outside of government, governmental agencies, and governmental funding. The Veejack religion must not be taught in public schools, advocated by governmental social services agencies, or promulgated within government offices, workspaces, or through events funded by the government.[32] The Veejack religion is no less important than other religions, but the Veejack religion's spiritual beliefs and practices should not be mandated and governmentally advocated to an unknowing, and unwilling populace.

Theologians and academics have consistently missed or ignored the emergence of the Veejack religion as, over the last fifty years, the embryonic Veejack religious faith matured from a barely known sect into a widely practiced and recognizable religion. Theologians have mistaken the lip service of some Veejackian proponents to Judeo-Christian rituals as a real adherence to the Judeo-Christian faith. But paying lip service to Judeo-Christian beliefs and participating in Judeo-Christian holiday rituals are not a substitute for faith.

---

[32] The importance of public schools as fertile ground for political socialization of young minds has long been recognized. See, e.g., Simon, James and Merrill, Bruce, "Political socialization in the classroom revisited: the Kids Voting program," *The Social Science Journal* v. 35 no1 (1998) p. 29-42, discussed at https://www2.lewisu.edu/~gazianjo/political_socialization_in_the_c.htm. The review notes that "American schools have long been viewed as agents of political socialization, helping to build support for the prevailing societal norms. Along with family, friends, the surrounding environment and the mass media, schools are seen as a major influence on young people as they develop a political awareness." See, also, Hernandez, Samantha, "Investigating How Politics Is Affecting Education? Here's What to Know," September 13, 2022, at https://ewa.org/news-explainers/how-politics-affects-education. One of the speakers featured at the educator's gathering stated the often-overlooked truism that "Public schooling is always political. It's shaped by politics." See, also, Zummo, Lynne, "Stanford education scholar explores how political views influence teens' understanding of climate change," April 21, 2020, at https://ed.stanford.edu/news/stanford-education-scholar-explores-how-political-views-influence-teens-understanding-climate. See, also, Walker, Tim, "'Education is Political': Neutrality in the Classroom Shortchanges Students – Discussing human rights and equity should be welcomed in classrooms, not dismissed as 'partisanship' or 'politics'", December 11, 2018, at https://www.nea.org/nea-today/all-news-articles/education-political-neutrality-classroom-shortchanges-students.

The Veejack religion encourages its members to observe the rituals of Judeo-Christian or other faiths but does not allow its followers to accept any of the doctrines or canons of these religions if they conflict with the Veejack religion's doctrines or canons. Catholic prelates have even coined the term "Cafeteria Catholics" for this behavior.[33] The Veejack religion's enthusiasts who profess allegiance to Catholicism believe they can treat the Catholic faith like a buffet and pick and choose which of the Catholic teachings they support. They reject the Catholic teachings to which they do not agree without recognizing that in so doing, they have abandoned the Catholic faith and been converted to the Veejack religion.

Philosopher Charles Taylor, writing in 2007 in his influential publication *A Secular Age*, observed that, "in earlier societies, religion was everywhere," but in modern times our "public spaces . . . have been . . . emptied of God, or of any reference to ultimate reality."[34] Taylor, while noting the absence of God and religion in public spaces, thought that people were losing their religious beliefs and practices. Taylor did not recognize that a new religion, in the form of the Veejack religion, was converting multitudes of people without their knowledge, and was becoming more prevalent in public spaces than any previous religion in the United States. Taylor did recognize, however, that society was moving from a firm belief in God to a belief that God is but one of many religious options. What Taylor failed to recognize was that the Veejack religion is one of the religious options; and, as a government-sponsored religion it has been encouraged by too many governmental, or government-funded, organizations.

Theologian Sandra Marie Schneiders, however, grasped the outlines of how the Veejack religion was able to secure itself such a prized place in society. She recognized as early as 2003 that traditional religions were being banished from public spaces. Without realizing

---

[33] A cafeteria Catholic is a follower of Catholicism who dissents from certain official doctrinal or moral teachings of the Catholic Church. See, e.g., https://en.wikipedia.org/wiki/Cafeteria_Catholicism

[34] Charles Taylor, *A Secular Age*, Cambridge, MA: Belknap Press, 2007, 2.

that the Veejack religion was lurking in the background as a nascent state-sponsored religion, Professor Schneiders wrote that "in the United States . . . the banishing of all religions as institutions from public life under a (mis)interpretation of the First Amendment has created a spiritual vacuum in which shared beliefs and values cannot be called upon to shape public policy or sanction private behavior."[35] Sadly, there was a religion – the Veejack religion – that was, and is, shaping public policy and sanctioning private behavior. And, too often, the public policy that it is shaping and the behavior it is sanctioning, include the rejection of traditional Judeo-Christian beliefs, practices, and art.

The purpose of this disclosure and discussion of the existence of the Veejack religion as an active, thriving, and powerful religion is not meant to suppress the practice of the Veejack religion or to demean its practitioners. Instead, it is to alert the citizens of the various states that the courts and legislators within the Federal, State, and local levels of government are actively supporting the practice of the Veejack religion. While banning the teaching of Judeo-Christian literature, practices, art, poetry, song, and symbology in public education and government funding, the public educational institutions and activities funded by the government actively proselytize the literature, practices, art, poetry, song, and symbology inherent in the Veejack religion.

The citizenry must no longer tolerate the Veejack religion being taught within public schools, social services, or governmental offices. It must no longer be acceptable for government policy to foster the Veejack religious indoctrination that results in schoolteachers "converting" young people to the Veejack religion and/or criticizing recognized faiths such as Judaism and Christianity. Indoctrination within the public schools by Veejack religion-inspired educators has

---

[35] Sandra Marie Schneiders, writing in "Religion vs. Spirituality: A Contemporary Conundrum", *Spiritus: A Journal of Christian Spirituality*, Vol 3, No 2, Fall 2003, 163-185, at 171.

been one of the most powerful methods for convincing young people to disaffiliate from Judaism and Christianity.

Federal, State, and local levels of government must stop advocating for the Veejack religion and eliminate the sanctioning of the Veejack religion in the same manner that they don't teach, or sanction within the schools or government, the practices of Judaism, Christianity, Islam, Latter-Day Saints, Native American religious beliefs, Druidry, Wicca, Rastafari, Druze, Buddhism, Hinduism, and other faiths. Federal, State, and local levels of government must cease to adopt the Veejack religion's doctrines, practices, vocabulary, penalties, and punishments where they exist within schools or governments. Federal, State, and local levels of government must eliminate the practices of the Veejack religion where they currently exist in the nation's public schools, governmental organizations, funding methods and agencies, and elsewhere.

The Veejack religion has accepted two main apocalypses into its creed. The first apocalypse was predicted in the late 19th century by revolutionary socialist Karl Marx. Marx's prediction of apocalypse was that the "state" – the civil governments – would, under the stresses of capitalism and industrialization, wither away and be replaced by a dictatorship of the people. As time has passed, and the capitalist first-world civil governments have shown no sign of withering away, the Veejack religion's elites developed the theory of a second apocalypse: the earth being destroyed by the use of carbon for fuel, synthetic materials, and other uses.

For the carbon apocalypse, the ordinary perturbations of systemic and changing weather patterns are harnessed into a mythology of catastrophic consequences.[36] These catastrophic consequences will occur if the people of the first world do not curb their consumption of carbon. Historically, the earth has been warming since the end of the last ice age approximately twelve thousand years ago. Beginning two and a half million years ago, the Pleistocene epoch covered the

---

[36] See, infra, Chapter Seven "Climate and the Weather Gods."

surface of the earth with glaciers of frozen water. Notwithstanding the adverse cold and icy conditions, it was during this period that *homo sapiens* evolved and spread across the earth. The Pleistocene epoch was followed by the Hôlocene epoch, in which we are living today.

Climate epochs occur because of the changing of the earth's position relative to the sun and other geomagnetic and solar system gravitational factors. The earth's orbit around the sun varies on a ninety-six-thousand-year cycle and the earth is cooler when it is further from the sun. As the Pleistocene epoch ended the glaciers began to melt, and the seas began to rise. The earth is continuing to warm as the Holocene epoch continues the warming trend.

The Veejack religion's propagandists, however, argue that humankind's – especially capitalist first-world countries' – use of carbon is the real cause of what they alternatively refer to as "global warming" during years of warmer weather, or as "climate change" during years in which the temperatures are cooler. The term global warming was a key component of the Veejack religion's teaching in the early twenty-first century. Still, when several years of cooler weather cast doubt on the Veejack religion's apocalyptic teachings, the more convenient and ubiquitous rubric of "climate change" was adopted.

The Veejack religion's new nomenclature of using the phrase "climate change" enables the Veejack religion to cast any significant weather alteration, no matter how historically common, as evidence of the apocalyptic changing of the climate – which they believe will lead inevitably to the destruction of the earth. That is, the earth will be destroyed unless the Veejack religion is able to harness its political power and force the people of the United States to eliminate the use of carbon, or exact huge fees from the populace for its continued use of carbon as a fuel, etc.

The Veejack religion's theory that successful capitalist countries are to blame for changes in the weather, no matter how ludicrous, permits the Veejack religion to criticize and penalize the United

States; while doing nothing to eliminate the enormous amounts of carbon emitted into the atmosphere by non-first-world nations like Russia, China, and India. This is evidence that the Veejack religion clings to its apocalyptic vision as a method of controlling the people of the United States and a formula for imposing its vision of a socialist dictatorship on the United States.

One of the dangerous practices of the Veejack religion is to proselytize itself without identifying its inherent characteristics as a religion. Accordingly, many of the most ardent practitioners of the Veejack religion do not recognize that they have been converted to the new religion. Many believe they are still practicing Jews, Christians,[37] Muslims, Buddhists, or other faiths; and many believe they are agnostic, atheist, or completely non-religious.[38] As will be

---

[37] For example, former Speaker of the United States House of Representative, Nancy Pelosi, professes that she is a devout Catholic even after being barred from receiving Holy Communion because of her support for abortion, which is opposed by the Catholic church. See, e.g., Shaw, Adam, "San Francisco archbishop bars Pelosi from receiving Holy Communion due to abortion support – Pelosi has said she is a 'devout' Catholic despite her abortion advocacy," May 20, 2022, at https://www.foxnews.com/politics/san-francisco-archbishop-pelosi-communion-abortion-support. And Roman Catholic Cardinal Wilton Gregory, archbishop of Washington, D.C., referred to President Biden as a "Cafeteria Catholic" who despite claiming to be a "devout Catholic", manipulates "dimensions of his faith for his 'political advantage'." Halon, Yael, "DC archbishop jabs Biden as 'cafeteria Catholic' who 'picks and chooses' for his 'political advantage' – Biden has repeatedly described himself as a 'devout Catholic' who attends church regularly," April 1, 2024 at https://www.foxnews.com/media/dc-archbishop-jabs-biden-cafeteria-catholic-who-picks-chooses-political-advantage. See, also, Hagstrom, Anders, "Catholic voters respond after 'devout' Biden once again sides against his Church," April 11, 2024 at https://www.foxnews.com/politics/catholic-voters-respond-devout-biden-once-sides-his-church. President Biden has even been criticized by Catholic Bishop Robert Gruss of Saginaw, Michigan for "supporting abortion, gender ideology, and other policies contrary to Church teaching". Bishop Gruss urges forgiveness, and states "I don't have any anger towards the president. I feel sorry for him. I'm not angry at him . . .." See, Nerozzi, Timothy, "Biden 'doesn't understand the Catholic faith,'. . .." April 20, 2024, at https://www.foxnews.com/faith-values/biden-doesnt-understand-catholic-faith-bishop-not-angry-him-hes-just-stupid

[38] Atheism is, as Hoffer points out at 86, a religion. Hoffer writes that "the atheist is a religious person . . . (who) believes in atheism as though it were a new religion . . .

discussed, *infra*, the Veejack religion is an atheistic faith that does not recognize a supreme being. However, its leaders do not object to, and even encourage, its followers professing an adherence to a supreme being so long as the Veejack religious follower adheres to the fundamental beliefs, practices, rituals, penalties, and punishments within the Veejack religion. Strikingly, because it is a religion, the Veejack faith does not permit compromise on quintessential issues and its adherents who dare to express independent thoughts or deviate from doctrine promulgated by its leaders are often severely rebuked, shunned, or punished by other members.[39]

Although this initial attempt is to identify and categorize the Veejack faith as a religion it should not be viewed as a comprehensive survey of the Veejack faith. As with the development of other religions, the Veejack faith's religious practices may take hundreds of years to solidify into their final form(s) and there may be schisms, sects, factions, and divisions within the Veejack faith that are never resolved. This discussion is just the starting point for recognizing the Veejack faith. Creative theologians, scholars, philosophers, historians, intellectuals, and other interested thinkers are invited to contribute to the literature and understanding of the Veejack faith as it evolves as a religion.

There must be further thoughtful, careful, and compassionate consideration of how to both protect the Veejack religious faith from oppression and protect the First Amendment proscription against the government establishing Veejack as a religion. Citizens and

---

(and) is an atheist with devoutness and unction." See, also, Dostoyevsky, "The Idiot", 1918, London: William Heinemann, Moulin Digital Editions, 2023, available at https://ia601600.us.archive.org/35/items/dostoyevsky_fyodor_1821_1881_idiot/dostoyevsky_fyodor_1821_1881_idiot.pdf, 455 where it reads: "And Russians do not merely become atheists, but they invariably believe in atheism, as though it were a new religion without noticing that they are putting faith in a negation."

[39] The public dialogues and discourses of Veejack's leaders often change abruptly as elections remove them from, or place them into, public office or appointed policy positions. It takes times for the evolving messaging to solidify and become known to the Veejack congregants.

especially parents must petition the legislative and judicial branches of government to eliminate the Veejack religion's teachings and beliefs from governmental organizations and funding and prevent its further propagation as a state-sponsored religion.

CHAPTER ONE

THE BEGINNINGS AND FORMATIONS OF RELIGIONS

The study of comparative theology, in which the student explores multiple religions to ascertain the similarities and differences is profoundly exciting. For example, the Judeo-Christian Bible's wisdom is as much in its collectivity and comprehending God's message, as it is within its individual passages. The ultimate Judeo-Christian concern is whether a person's acts and deeds comply with God's law. When faced with a critical choice or dilemma the Judeo-Christian practice is to pray; to seek God's guidance. When in a crisis or dangerous situation the Judeo-Christian plea is for God's intervention, protection, and mercy. If a person commits an act that violates God's law the wrongdoer asks for God's forgiveness.

Hindu literature offers its own unique path to understanding and bonding with God. The Bible and Hindu literature differ in approach to seeking God and enlightenment. The differences in the approaches may be due to the dissimilar cultural and physical environments of the Indian subcontinent and the Middle East. What is similar is that within both cultures the people are seeking a connection to, and understanding of, their relationship with God.

Hinduism

Although western writers commonly refer to the non-Islamic religions in India as "Hinduism", there is not a unified religious system or tradition named "Hinduism".[40] The term "Hinduism" was "derived from a name applied by foreigners to the people living in the region of the Indus River, and was introduced in the nineteenth century under the colonial British rule as a category for census-taking."[41] It has been argued that:

> Western analysis of Hinduism has been carried on by outsiders who were biased against Indian culture, or who presumed that all religions can be studied according to Western religious categories. Even the Hindi word "dharma," often translated into English simply as "religion," refers to a broad complex of meanings, encompassing duty, natural law, social welfare, ethics, health, wealth, power, fulfillment of desires, and transcendental realization. Furthermore, Hinduism is not easily separated fully from other dharmic traditions that have arisen in India, including Buddhism, Jainism, and Sikhism, for there has been extensive cross-pollination among them.[42]

---

[40] Fisher, 71.

[41] Fisher, 71. As with the derivation of the term "Hinduism" as applied by a foreign occupying power, the term Veejack is equally appropriate as a sobriquet for those individuals in the United States that subscribe to the socialist-derived religion of views inconsistent with Judeo-Christian theology.

[42] Fisher, 71. Criticism of Veejack as an outsider's view may be both supported and challenged by this passage. Although not a Veejackian, the author of this book is intimately familiar with the history and growth of the Veejack religion. Veejack must be studied in a Western religious tradition because it is the Western concept of freedom of religion and its implementation in the First Amendment to the United States Constitution that is at issue. To view Veejack as separate from the "broad complex of meanings, encompassing duty, natural law, social welfare, ethics, health,

In actuality, the people of India are multireligious with practices that range from ascetism to sensuality. Some believe in a deity, some in multiple deities, and others support theories of abstract ideas and/or the "oneness behind the material world."[43] In other words, there is not one set of beliefs that define Hinduism.[44] Much of the diversity within the religious beliefs in India is due to the millennia within which the various religious practices have had time to penetrate various ranges of geography and society.

Most Western readers are more familiar with the popular conception that Hinduism is coterminous with Brahmanism. The Brahminic tradition goes back thousands of years to the Dravidian peoples and the cities that grew in the Indus Valley three to four thousand years ago. Brahmanism has philosophical and metaphysical aspects, as well as devotional and ritualistic practices that, woven together, have evolved into a cultural pattern. This culture, however, was believed to have been overrun by invaders. And the invaders are believed to be the authors of "the Vedas, the religious texts often referred to as the foundations of Hinduism . . . (which) were the product of the invaders and not of indigenous Indians, or perhaps a combination of both cultures."[45]

The invasion theory does not have universal scholarly support, and many academics believe the Vedas were produced by agricultural or pastoral peoples, rather than by the urban-centered Indus Valley culture.[46] Notwithstanding that the Vedas are wrapped in the smoky cloak of antiquity, they are vibrant and considered to be:

wealth, power, fulfillment of desires, and transcendental realization" that make up the Veejack faith would be to stand the First Amendment on its head as an imposition of religion by the government.

[43] Fisher, 71.

[44] This is true as well for the Veejack faith, where there are many competing and even contradictory sects and factions within the religion of Veejack.

[45] Fisher, 72.

[46] Fisher, 72-73. Fisher, at 74, provides a timeline that dates the Vedas as within the oral tradition beginning as early as 8,000 BCE, but not written down until sometime between 3100 BCE and 900 BCE. This wide diversity shows how little is known about the evolution and growth of the Brahminic practices.

shruti texts—those which have been revealed, rather than written by mortals. They are the breath of the eternal, as "heard" by the ancient sages, or rishis, and later compiled by Vyasa. The name "Vyasa" means "Collector." He was traditionally considered to be one person, but some scholars think it likely that many people were acting as compilers.[47]

An interesting aspect of the pastoral agricultural tradition is the unique representation of trees.[48] This is especially true for the peepul tree, which is considered sacred and used as a place of worship.[49] The use of indoor structures for worship seems to have evolved later although outdoor festivals, parades, and gatherings are still the norm.[50] One of the most oft-repeated Vedas has a verse, known as the *Gayatrimantra*, that celebrates the creative hum of the universe. It celebrates the earth, atmosphere, and heaven, the adoration of glory, splendor and grace that radiate from the Divine light that illuminates earth, atmosphere, and heaven, and a prayer requesting the "light of universal intelligence."[51]

---

[47] Fisher, 75.

[48] Fisher, 85.

[49] Fisher, 73. See, also, https://en.wikipedia.org/wiki/Ficus_religiosa:
Ficus religiosa or sacred fig is a species of fig native to the Indian subcontinent and Indochina that belongs to Moraceae, the fig or mulberry family. It is also known as the bodhi tree, peepul tree, peepal tree, pipala tree or ashvattha tree (in India and Nepal). The sacred fig is considered to have a religious significance in three major religions that originated on the Indian subcontinent, Hinduism, Buddhism and Jainism. Hindu and Jain ascetics consider the species to be sacred and often meditate under it. Gautama Buddha is believed to have attained enlightenment under a tree of this species. The sacred fig is the state tree of the Indian states of Odisha, Bihar and Haryana.

[50] The practice of outdoor services is also a well-known feature of the Veejack faith. The Veejack religion employs street marches, demonstrations outside of government facilities and other buildings, and outdoor festivals to generate publicity, bolster its adherents, and recruit new members.

[51] Fisher, 75.

Another Veda, the *Rig Veda*, praises and implores the blessings of the *devas* [52] which control the cosmos and consecrate every aspect of a person's life.[53] For example:

> The major devas included *Indra* (god of thunder and bringer of welcome rains), *Agni* (god of fire), *Soma* (associated with a sacred drink), and *Ushas* (goddess of dawn). The devas included both opaque earth gods and transparent deities of the sky and celestial realms. But behind all the myriad aspects of divinity, the sages perceived one unseen reality. This reality, beyond human understanding, ceaselessly creates and sustains everything that exists, encompassing all time, space, and causation.[54]

In addition to the *Rig Veda* there are three other collections of hymns and sacred sounds that are recited while making offerings to the deities and lighting sacred fires.[55]

---

[52] *Deva* means "shiny", "exalted", "heavenly being", "divine being", "anything of excellence", and is also one of the Sanskrit terms used to indicate a deity in Hinduism. *Deva* is a masculine term; the feminine equivalent is *Devi*. The word is a cognate with Latin *deus* ("god") and Greek Zeus. See, e.g., https://en.wikipedia.org/wiki/Deva_ (Hinduism).

[53] Fisher, 75.

[54] Fisher, 75-76.

[55] Fisher, 76 and 83. The Veejack religion has its equivalent of sacred sounds in the use of group chants of rhyming couplets that bolster the Veejack adherents' *esprit de corps* and intimidate their opponents as they march, demonstrate, or congregate near their opponents. The origin of Veejack's use of rhyming couplets is unknown but goes back decades if not centuries. Many are gaining the status of tradition. Others have a fleeting existence as they are spontaneously created during Veejack street-oriented religious events and then wafted like smoke through throngs of Veejack worshippers as they march. Many spontaneous chants are captured by press members or "influencers" sympathetic to Veejack and then shared state-wide or even nationally via television or electronic media.

Other ancient *shruti* texts include the *Brahmanas* (directions about performances of the ritual sacrifices to the deities), *Aranyakas* ("forest treatises" by sages who went to the forests to meditate as recluses), and Upanishads (teachings from highly realized spiritual masters). The principal Upanishads are thought to have developed last, around 600 to 100 BCE. They represent the mystical insights of rishis who sought ultimate reality through their meditations in the forest. Many people consider these philosophical and metaphysical reflections the cream of Indian thought, among the highest spiritual literature ever written. They were not taught to the masses but rather were reserved for advanced seekers of spiritual truth. Emphasis is placed not on outward ritual performances, as in the earlier texts, but on inner experience as the path to realization and immortality.[56]

The separation of the elites from the masses was a significant step toward minority participation in the Braminic tradition. Prior to 600 CE manual laborers and women were excluded from spiritual expression.[57] However, around 600 CE a ritual and philosophic approach known as *bhakti* became popular and the caste that included manual laborers and women were allowed to participate.[58]

---

[56] Fisher, 76. Interestingly, one aspect of the Veejack faith that mimics the *Brahmanas* is the separation in status of the leadership, who are taught the existing texts, and create the new texts, of Veejackism from the masses, who are not. Within Veejackism the practice appears to be to maintain the masses at a semi-literate level so that they are unlikely to deviate from the Veejack's message *du jour*. The Veejackian leaders tend to send their children to elite private educational institutions while keeping the children of the masses in mediocre public institutions that are more indoctrination centers than they are spaces of learning.

[57] Fisher, 83.

[58] Fisher, at 98, explains that included at the top of the caste system are priests and philosophers known as brahmins, next were the Kshatriyas who were the nobility

The Brahminic tradition has a practice of emitting sacred sounds as a meditative practice that leads to a higher state of consciousness.[59] In the state of higher consciousness the practitioner hopes to experience an infinite reality beyond the five senses.[60] The *dharmic*[61] tradition posits that the cosmos is unified with the reality exposed by the five human senses and connected. This is the "unseen but all pervading reality Brahman, the Unknowable: 'Him the eye does not see, nor the tongue express, nor the mind grasp.'"[62]

The goal for the practitioners is to discover the inner self, known as the *atman*,[63] and by merging with its transcendence to experience "unspeakable peace and bliss."[64] Most religions contemplate the uniquely human inquiry of what happens after a person dies. For Hindus, one of the central doctrines of the Upanishads is

---

and warriors, then came the farmers and merchants, and at the bottom were the "untouchables" comprised of manual laborers and artisans. Caste membership was hereditary and there was little social contact between the castes. Unlike within the Hindu caste system, which relegates artisans to the lowest caste, the religion of Veejack economically rewards its top musicians, artists, and creative writers. However, the religion of Veejack has a politically favored but economically disadvantaged caste composed of those who receive public assistance and dwell in public housing or live as unhoused street dwellers. Within this group are semi-nomadic facilitators who travel on short notice to assist Veejack elites that require aggression during demonstrations, marches, and other events.

[59] Fisher, 76. The Veejack faith, as will be noted *infra*, also has "sacred sounds." Veejack's sacred sounds are usually in the form of often ecstatic rhyming chants that are collectively shouted during their group marches and stationary gatherings.

[60] Fisher, 76.

[61] Dharma is a key concept with multiple meanings in the Indian religions (Hinduism, Buddhism, Jainism, and Sikhism), among others. Although no single-word translation exists for *dharma* in English (or other European languages), the term is commonly understood as referring to behaviors that are in harmony with the "order and custom" that sustain life; "virtue", or "religious and moral duties". See e.g., https://en.wikipedia.org/wiki/Dharma.

[62] Fisher, 77.

[63] *Ātman* is a Sanskrit word for the true or eternal Self or the self-existent essence of each individual, which persists across multiple bodies and lifetimes. See, e.g., https://en.wikipedia.org/wiki/%C4%80tman_(Hinduism).

[64] Fisher, 77.

reincarnation.[65] In their view, upon the death of the body the soul leaves the dead body and enters a new body. Their understanding is that the soul:

> takes birth again and again in countless bodies—perhaps as an animal or some other life form—but the self remains the same. Birth as a human being is a precious and rare opportunity for the soul to advance toward its ultimate goal of liberation from rebirth and merging with the Absolute Reality.[66]

A related insight is the concept of *Karma*.[67] *Karma* relates to human action and the outcomes that result from human actions. It is understood that every human act has a consequence and shapes the future. In other words, the outcome of life is made by the human being living the life. Pure deeds result in a pure person, and impure deeds lead to an impure life. As author of theology texts Mary Pat Fisher explains, *Karma* is a concept of "(n)ot only do we reap in this life the good or evil we have sown; they also follow us after physical death, affecting our next incarnation. Ethically, this is a strong teaching, for our every move has far-reaching consequences."[68] The objective is not to create good lives through good deeds, but to breakout of the endless cycle of birth, death, and rebirth, known as Samsara.[69] As Fisher explains:

---

[65] Fisher, 77.

[66] Fisher, 77.

[67] Karma is a concept of action, work, or deed, and its effect or consequences. In Indian religions, the term more specifically refers to a principle of cause and effect, often descriptively called the principle of karma, wherein individuals' intent and actions (cause) influence their future (effect): Good intent and good deeds contribute to good karma and happier rebirths, while bad intent and bad deeds contribute to bad karma and bad rebirths. See, e.g., https://en.wikipedia.org/wiki/Karma.

[68] Fisher, 77.

[69] Fisher, 77.

(t)o escape from samsara is to achieve moksha, or liberation from the limitations of space, time, and matter through realization of the immortal Absolute. Many lifetimes of upward-striving incarnations are required to reach this transcendence of earthly miseries. This desire for liberation from earthly existence is one of the underpinnings of classical Hinduism . . ..[70]

In addition to the *Vedas*, the Braminic religions originating on the Indian subcontinent developed sophisticated systems of philosophy. One of the key traditions was that ethics were essential for an orderly social life.[71]

The feminine aspect of the divine is worshipped by approximately fifty million Hindus, and the divine worship of a feminine goddess dates to pre-*Vedic* ancient peoples.[72] The worship of a goddess takes many forms. The power of the goddess is known as *shakti* and represents a cosmic energy of dynamic forces that penetrate the universe.[73] As described by Sri Swami Sivananda it is natural to regard the divine as a mother, because:

---

[70] Fisher, 77. The religion of Veejack, as previously noted, in nontheistic. The religion of Veejack does not have corollary practices like the Brahmic concepts of *atman*, reincarnation, *dharma*, or *karma*. Instead, individual members of the Veejack religion are permitted to hold a variety of beliefs provided that those beliefs do not conflict with direct Veejack teachings. This is because Veejack leaders recognize such belief facilitates the stealth attribute of Veejackism by allowing individual members to believe within themselves that they are actually followers of a different religion such as Judaism, Islam, Christianity, Buddhism, Hinduism, etc.

[71] Fisher, 78. The centrality of ethics as essential for an orderly social life is absent from the teachings of the Veejack religion. Veejack has situational ethics inculcating an ethical structure that accepts a doctrine of flexibility of moral laws according to the circumstances. Situational ethics or situation ethics considers only the context of an act when evaluating it ethically, rather than judging it only according to absolute moral standards. See, e.g., https://en.wikipedia.org/wiki/Situational_ethics.

[72] Fisher, 84.

[73] https://en.wikipedia.org/wiki/Shakti. Veejack is a nontheistic religion that does not recognize gods or goddesses however one of its most progressive aspects is the

To the child, in the mother is centered a whole world of tenderness, of love, of nourishment and of care. It is the ideal world from where one draws sustenance, where one runs for comfort, which one clings to for protection and nourishment; and there he gets comfort, protection and care. Therefore, the ideal of love, care and protection is in the conception of the mother.[74]

The female deity, however, is not always gentle and may appear in a fierce form as well. The female goddess may be "portrayed dripping with blood, carrying a sword and a severed head, and wearing a girdle of severed hands and a necklace of skulls symbolizing her aspect as the destroyer of evil."[75] The female deity does not destroy but instead transforms. With her "merciful sword she cuts away all personal impediments to realization of truth for those who sincerely desire to serve the Supreme."[76] And she welcomes those who love her. While she was previously celebrated with animal blood offerings, the practice of religious animal sacrifices is ending "at the behest of animal lovers."[77] Although most sects celebrate

---

prominence of women in its leadership roles. As the Veejack religion grows and matures it will probably begin to celebrate its female heroes and will likely have its female heroes join Karl Marx, Friederich Engels, and Michael Harrington in its commemorative traditions.

[74] Fisher, 85

[75] Fisher, 85. Within the Veejack religion the feminine leadership often self-proclaim their fierce persona and wave weapons in the air as part of their projection of strength. In Veejack the projection of strength is frequently considered more important than having strength because faux projected strength is less expensive to generate and maintain and it tends to intimidate the foes of Veejack as well as actual strength.

[76] Fisher, 85.

[77] Fisher, 85. The protection of animals occupies a prominent place in many Veejack sects, and is generally given at least lip-service respect by almost all Veejack sects. The power of Veejack to impact the culture of the United States is exemplified by its opposition to wearing garments of animal fur. Prior to the late 20th century, the wearing of animal fur was a sign of status. Then Veejack's animal rights activists challenged the wearing of animal fur on ethical grounds and often splashed paint on

the spiritual nature of the feminine, some sects celebrate its worldly aspects. As Fisher notes, some "subvert orthodox Hindu notions of purity and impurity through the use of . . . meat, fish, parched grain, wine, and sexual intercourse in which the woman is worshiped as the goddess."[78] However, this practice is considered reserved for "advanced initiates".[79]

Buddhism

There are also religions that have no conception of a god. For example, Buddhism, the name given to the religion of the people that follow Buddha's teachings, is a nontheistic religion. The religion has no personal god and Buddha is not considered to have been, or become, a god. However, Buddha "attained full enlightenment through meditation and . . . (developed a) path of spiritual awakening and freedom" for his disciples to follow.[80] Unlike with many other religious traditions, Buddha did not propound a theory on the creation of the universe, describe unseen realities like heaven or hell, express the nature of the human soul, or visualize an afterlife. Instead, Buddha taught wisdom, enlightenment, and compassion; and that "salvation and enlightenment are available . . . through removal of defilements and delusion and a life of meditation".[81]

"Buddha" was born in what is now northern India in the fifth century BCE. His name was Siddhartha Gautama. Legend says his mother, Maya, gave birth in a garden; and some Buddhists believe he

---

people wearing animal fur. Because of Veejack's actions the practice of wearing animal fur is no longer fashionable in the United States.

[78] Fisher, 86.

[79] Fisher, 86. Within the Veejack religion hedonistic practices are generally the province of the elites.

[80] Fisher, Mary Pat in "Living Religions", Chapter 5 "Buddhism", 143. *Living Religions*, Ninth Edition, by Mary Pat Fisher. Published by Pearson. Copyright © 2014 by Pearson Education, Inc.

[81] Fisher, 143.

was conceived when a white elephant carrying a lotus flower entered Maya's womb. [82]

The stories of Buddha say that his father was a wealthy man, and the chief of the Shakyas, one of the Kshatriya clans. Gautama was raised in luxury, with mansions, a harem, wife, and son. Despite his wealth and position he was shocked when he saw a "bent old man, a sick person, a dead person, and . . . (a person) seeking lasting happiness rather than . . . pleasure".[83] After seeing these four images and determining their significance as the shortness of life, suffering, old age, and death Buddha, at the age of 29, renounced his wealth, left his wife and son, shaved his head, wore a coarse robe, and became an ascetic seeking a way to be liberated from suffering.

After enduring suffering, he began teaching. He became known as Shakyamuni Buddha the "sage of the Shakya clan".[84] His core teachings, known as the Dharma, included the Four Noble Truths, the Noble Eightfold Path, the Three Marks of Existence, and other lessons that were passed orally for several generations. Buddha's teachings were not reduced to writing for several hundred years.[85]

The Four Noble Truths are that life involves suffering, dissatisfaction, and distress (known as *dukkha*); that *dukkha* is caused by craving, rooted in ignorance; that *dukkha* will cease when craving ceases; and, by following the Noble Eightfold Path of ethical conduct, concentration and wisdom, a person can obtain the desired state.[86] The Eightfold Path consists of "right" things: understanding,

---

[82] Fisher, 138.

[83] Fisher, 138.

[84] Fisher, 140.

[85] The early stages of Buddhism are like the current condition of Veejack. Veejack has no commonly accepted texts, path to enlightenment, or characteristics. This may be, in part, to the evolving nature of Veejack or to its propensity to change its views depending on the economic, social, or political conditions.

[86] Fisher, 144-145. Veejack shares with Buddhism the belief that life involves suffering and distress. But unlike Buddhism, which attributes it to personal craving, Veejack absolves its practitioners of personal responsibility and blames racism, homophobia, or another amorphous societal attribute.

thought, speech, action, livelihood (line of work that does not violate the "right" precepts), eliminating impurities, mindfulness, and meditation. The Three Marks (or characteristics) of Existence are *dukkha, anicca* (impermanence) and *anatta* (no eternal self).

Buddhism is a nontheistic religion.[87] However Buddha, although not worshipped as a god, "attained full enlightenment through meditation and . . . (developed a) path of spiritual awakening and freedom" for his disciples to follow.[88] Unlike founders of other religious traditions, Buddha did not propound a theory on the creation of the universe, describe unseen realities like heaven or hell, express the nature of the human soul, or visualize an afterlife. Instead, as described by Buddhists who attended the 1993 Parliament of the World's Religions, Buddha taught wisdom, enlightenment, and compassion; and that "salvation and enlightenment are available . . . through removal of defilements and delusion and a life of meditation".[89]

Buddhism, as with many religions, has multiple traditions.[90]

---

[87] Veejack is also nontheistic. However, to disguise its presence and to attract to its teachings those that might otherwise shy away, Veejack permits its practitioners to claim allegiance to a theistic faith provided that the practitioner does not comply with the theistic faith's teachings if they conflict with Veejack orthodoxy.

[88] Fisher, 143.

[89] Fisher, 143.

[90] Veejack also has multiple traditions and sects. Opponents to Veejack's status as a religion may argue that its diversity belies it is a religion; however, since all religions have sects and schisms the diversity within Veejack merely shows the vitality and dynamism of the Veejack faith among its practitioners. Veejack often encourages its adherents to adopt Buddhist practices and style because they have an accepted religiosity that gives a patina of respectability. Even Catholicism accepts many Buddhist traits, provided they do not conflict with Catholic teachings. In the *Declaration on the Relation of the Church to Non-Christian Religions Nostra Aetate Proclaimed by His Holiness Pope Paul VI on October 28, 1965*, it states:
. . . Buddhism, in its various forms, realizes the radical insufficiency of this changeable world; it teaches a way by which . . . (people), in a devout and confident spirit, may be able either to acquire the state of perfect liberation, or attain, by their own efforts or through higher help, supreme illumination. *** The Catholic Church rejects nothing that is true and holy in . . . (Buddhism). She regards with sincere reverence those ways of conduct and of life, those precepts and teachings which, though differing in many

Buddhist scholar Thich Nhat Hanh observes that "(i)n Buddhism . . . there have been many schisms. One hundred years after . . . Buddha, the community of his disciples divided into two parts; within four hundred years there were twenty schools . . .."[91] For example, the Theravada tradition teaches that the person, Shakyamuni Buddha, taught the Dharma as a guide to liberation from suffering and, as with all people, died. Unlike the Theravada tradition, the Mahayana tradition believes Buddha embodied "enlightened awareness", is an "immanent presence", and has three aspects or "bodies":

> formless enlightened wisdom; a body of bliss that communicates with bodhisattvas (people dedicated to liberating others from suffering); and an emanation body in which Buddha appears to help liberate suffering beings.[92]

The Mahayana tradition also envisions the three aspects of Buddha as pure, with unlimited compassion, omniscient wisdom, enlightenment, and the capability to move through intergalactic space and time; and Buddha has the ability to appear in multiple places in multiple forms simultaneously. The most "complex and profound" of the Mahayana teachings is the "emptiness or voidness".[93] The belief referred to as the "emptiness or void" holds that nothing really exists; and all phenomena arise and pass away. Both the Theravada and Mahayana traditions share a belief that reality is not absolute, but impermanent; since all things arise and perish continuously, they do not really exist.[94]

---

aspects from the ones she holds and sets forth, nonetheless often reflect a ray of that Truth which enlightens all . . . (people).

[91] Hahn, Thich Nhat, *Living Buddha, Living Christ*, New York: Riverhead Books, 2007 (the text does not contain page numbers, so direct citation to pages cannot be accomplished).

[92] Fisher, 160.

[93] Fisher, 160.

[94] Fisher, 160.

However, there are other traditions in Buddhism that are more lighthearted. In Japan, Buddhists celebrate Shakyamuni's birthday in early April, coinciding with the blooming of cherry blossoms.[95] The festival is a happy celebration of the birth of the baby Buddha. This celebration is markedly different in contour and context from the more ascetic, austere practice of Buddhism in other countries.

Modern Buddhism continues to ponder current ethical issues, such as abortion, reproductive technologies, genetic engineering, suicide, and euthanasia, etc.[96] In this, and in many other ways, "Buddhism is . . . as relevant today . . . as in the sixth century BCE, when . . . Shakyamuni Buddha renounced a life of ease to save all sentient beings from suffering".[97]

Veejack Religious Concerns

The ultimate concern of Veejack's religious adherents is not whether God approves of their acts and deeds, or to seek spiritual enlightenment, but instead the Veejack religion's adherent's concern is whether their peers approve of their action. When faced with a critical choice or dilemma the Veejack religion's adherent's response is not to pray; instead, the Veejack religion's believer's response is to express rage, resort to violence, and denounce elected Judeo-Christian, political and/or commercial economic leaders. When an adherent of the Veejack religion is in a crises or dangerous situation the Veejack religious adherent's plea is not to God, but is instead directed to the media, peers within the Veejack religion, and supportive elected public officials.

---

[95] Veejack, too, has a Spring festival that is celebrated on May 1. Veejack's Spring Festival is alternatively known as International Workers' Day, or where its Marxist origins must be excluded (i.e., first recognized in the Marxist International Social Congress in 1889), as May Day.

[96] Fisher, 185.

[97] Fisher, 185.

Studying comparative theology offers a rewarding and challenging experience to explore various religious traditions.[98] It is eye opening to learn how various religions evolved from the ideas of one person or group of people and evolved into widely shared and accepted belief systems. For example, the Abrahamic faiths teach the existence of God, concepts of normative behaviors, respect for the natural environment, belief in an afterlife, and respect for spirituality. However, as Buddhism and the Veejack religion show, belief in a god is not a prerequisite for a religion to thrive.

Christianity is but one of the religions in the Abrahamic monotheistic tradition. Other Abrahamic traditions include Judaism and Islam. For Christians the primary area of study is the Bible's New Testament. The Christian Bible's Old Testament originated with Judaism's Hebrew Bible, called the Septuagint. Both the Christian and Jewish faiths use the Old Testament / Septuagint in their religious worship and its practitioners are familiar with its literature and teachings. The Islamic Quran (Koran) is the central religious text of Islam.

Comparative mysticism focuses on and posits that what lies on the surface of an ideology may be illusory and that the reality underneath may be both vast and unfathomable. There is reality below the conscious surface. The Veejack religion is misunderstood and unrecognized as it influences and overwhelmes public schools, higher educational institutions, and various governmental offices. It is not a passing fad. Instead, it is a multidimensional religious

---

[98] One goal is to explore other religions' concepts of eternity. Moses ben Maimon (Maimonides), a medieval Sephardic Jewish Torah scholar, observed that eternity is a dimension where time does not exist. The theory that "eternity is a place where time does not exist" is mentioned in passing in many sermons and teachings. And eternity was discussed in the works of theoretical physicist Brian Greene, whose writings explain theories about the universe to non-physicists. The mental exercise of trying to comprehend a dimension where time does not exist is exhausting. For example, is being alive in the present simultaneously a "hook" into always existing in the timeless eternal dimension. This circular equation positing that if time doesn't exist, and one is alive now, then one will always be alive is a quandary.

movement sweeping vast numbers of economically affluent and educationally advanced people into its folds, and also attracting the less affluent and those receiving government assistance.

Unexpectedly, gaining knowledge about, and insight into, religions such as Hinduism, Buddhism, Daoism and Confucianism illuminates this new religion known as Veejack. Obtaining knowledge on the beliefs, customs, practices, and growth of diverse self-acknowledged religions helps to recognize the beliefs, customs, practices, and growth of the stealth Veejack religion. Studying the Veejack faith as a religion throws open a window that looks out over the fields and sees the Veejack's religion's seeds sprouting in government, public education, and areas of commerce.

Christianity, a religion that grew from a persecuted minority and evolved into a powerful faith, is now seemingly in decline in the United States. The beliefs, practices, and leadership of the Veejack religion are challenging the Judeo-Christian theologies.[99]

---

[99] In some respects, Veejack's academic supporters, and some pseudo-Judeo-Christian leaders who fail to recognize they've adopted Veejack beliefs, try to argue that the Bible supports Veejackism. The Bible does not support having economic, academic, and political elites taking earnings from hard working individuals and dispensing the funds to their friends and favored individuals. These faux scholars of Judeo-Christian literature justify Veejack practices as, for example, supported by Jesus. Although Veejack's supporters among the Christian clergy have tried to portray Jesus as supporting Veejack theology, this view is wrong. Jesus' teachings do not support Veejackism. And Jesus was not a socialist. Jesus was a Jewish rabbi who articulated God's love and caring for all people. Matthew 26:49; Mark 9:5, 11:21, 14:45; John 1:38; 1:49. Veejack's supporters that are familiar with the Bible's New Testament point to the passages where Jesus allows his disciples to eat from farmers' fields as justifying theft without recognizing that travelers eating from farmer's fields and gleaners was sanctioned by Judaism. Mark 2:23-28. The "Jesus was a socialist" promoters argue that workers should share their earning with nonworkers because Jesus told the parable of the workers who were paid the same wage for fewer hours work as those that worked long hours. Matthew 20:1-16. It was not the government, but the individual employer who determined the equality of wages – and perhaps the employer offered the same wage as an incentive to hire because otherwise the crops would not have been harvested. And Jesus' praising the giving of gifts and funds to the poor was because the gifts were freely given and not mandated by the government.

Some authors even argue that Jesus was a socialist.[100] And since the proponents – possibly evangelists – of Veejack religion have free roam of public schools, higher education, and government the teachings of the Veejack religion are assuming the mantel of unchallengeable "truths". This is wrong. The Veejack religion should not have unfettered access to the minds of the young, the halls of government, or funding from the public purse.

Religions Morph

It would be a bridge too far to explore failed religions, but there are fascinating insights from studying the religions of Mesoamerica.[101] Although the Aztecs and their religion were overcome by the Spanish, some aspects of the Aztec religion were adopted and morphed into the Catholic religion that was adopted by the native population. The Aztec Catholics showed that a religion like Catholicism can absorb the concepts, holy sites, and beliefs of an earlier failed religion. There is a probability that the reverse is true: that individuals or groups, while presuming that they are remaining loyal to a preexisting faith, absorb new, even contrary, beliefs into their religion. That appears to be what is occurring with concepts of the Veejack religion that are being absorbed into various Judeo-Christian sects. Senior leaders of Judeo-Christian sects need to carefully challenge the Veejack religion's core beliefs as antithetical to the Judeo-Christian theological traditions.

As noted above, a religion does not have to believe in the existence of a supreme being. Buddhism offers insight into what a nontheistic

---

[100] Nihlean, Joel, "Can You Truly Be Christian Without Being Some Kind of Socialist? – Christianity and socialism share many overarching goals. When you look at these similarities, making the case the Christians ought to be socialists becomes pretty simple," June 22, 2021, at https://aninjusticemag.com/how-christianity-and-socialism-make-each-other-better-b988dd750fc6.

[101] Carrasco, David, *Religions in Mesoamerica*, 2nd ed., Long Grove, IL: Waveland Press, Inc., 2014.

religion believes. Questions include whether a nontheistic religion must hold collective meetings? Whether a nontheistic religion must accept the existence of an afterlife? Whether a nontheistic religion must have some sort of faith as a component; and if so, faith in what? Must a nontheistic religion seek some sort of truth; and if so, how would it define truth? And must a nontheistic religion impose normative behavioral models on its adherents; and, if so, from where would it derive the models? These questions offer a door to exploration of comparative religion, and they bring into focus the reality of Veejackism as a religion that, while still denying its own existence, has emerged as a powerful force within the United States.

Denial by its adherents that it is a religion may originate from a variety of reasons. Some religious practitioners, such as the 1st century Christians, did not know that they were practicing a new religion; and believed they were Jewish. Later, Christians and other religions, for reasons of safety or to avoid persecution, denied their own existence. The need to avoid persecution was true for early Christians in Nero's Rome, for Muslims when the Moors were driven from Spain, and for Jews during the Spanish Inquisition, Russian pogroms, and Nazi Holocaust. Thus, the Veejack religion's denial of its status as a religion may be caused by: 1) its practitioners' failure to recognize they are practicing the Veejack religion; 2) its practitioners recognize their undertakings and activities violate the First Amendment; or 3) they realize they could face ostracism and loss of status if their true affiliation with the Veejack religion were known to their family, friends, and/or colleagues.

CHAPTER TWO

FIRST AMENDMENT GUARANTEES AND PROTECTIONS

The United States is unique because it has no official religion and protects the right of all people to practice the religion of their choice.[102] The prohibition on establishment of an official religion and the guarantee of the right of each person to practice a religion of their choice are enshrined in the First Amendment to the Constitution of the United States. The language on religion in the First Amendment is simple. It reads: "Congress shall make no law respecting an establishment of religion, or prohibiting the free exercise thereof."[103] These two clauses are referred to as the "establishment clause" and the "free exercise clause."[104]

Although the First Amendment originally applied only to the Federal government, the free exercise clause now applies to the actions of state governments through the due process clause of the

---

[102] See, e.g., H.R.1308 – Religious Freedom Restoration Act of 1993, enacted as Public Law No.: 103-141, and codified at 42 U.S.C. § 2000bb et seq.

[103] U S Const. Amend. 1.

[104] Erwin Chemerinsky, Constitutional Law – Principles and Policies, 6th Ed., (New York: Wolters Kluwer), 2019, 1294.

Fourteenth Amendment to the Constitution.[105] The establishment clause was later also determined to apply to state governments.[106] The two-fold protection of religion in the First Amendment – one prohibiting the government from establishing a required religion and the other protecting the right to practice religion – combine to produce the unique religious liberty available within the United States. These protections are necessary. For, as the Supreme Court has said, a "state-created orthodoxy puts at grave risk that freedom of belief and conscience which are the sole assurance that religious faith is real, not imposed."[107] That the Veejack religion has assumed the status of a state-created orthodoxy is a frightening menace that is hanging above American society like a sword of Damocles and is curtailing the religious freedom of millions of Americans.[108]

That these two protections work together is explained by Constitutional law scholar Erwin Chemerinsky. Chemerinsky writes, "if the state were to create a religion and compel participation, it obviously would be establishing a religion and, at the same time, denying free exercise to those who did not want to participate in religion or who wished to choose a different faith."[109] Chemerinsky's fear is exactly what is occurring in the United States as the Veejack religion, through its required instruction in the schools, mandated training and adherence in Federal and state government offices, and

---

[105] Chemerinsky, 1294, citing *Cantwell v. Connecticut*, 310 U.S. 296 (1940). Please note that decisions of the Supreme Court of the United States are cited with the volume number, the abbreviation "U.S." and then the page number on which the legal opinion begins.

[106] Chemerinsky, 1294, citing *Everson v. Board of Education*, 330 U.S. 1 (1947).

[107] Chemerinsky, 1294, quoting from *Lee v. Weisman*, 505 U.S. 577, 592 (1992). When quoting specific language from a legal opinion, the relevant page number(s) for the quote follow the number of the page that begins the opinion.

[108] See, e.g., Hirst, K. Kris, "What Did Cicero Mean by the Sword of Damocles? - A Roman Moral Philosophy on How to Be Happy", ThoughtCo, April 12, 2018, at https://www.thoughtco.com/what-is-the-sword-of-damocles-117738. Hirst explains that "The 'sword of Damocles' . . . means a sense of impending doom, the feeling that there is some catastrophic threat looming over you".

[109] Chemerinsky, 1295.

funding programs that channel billions of dollars into the Veejack religion's nonprofit organizations, is a compelled religion.

The conundrum for scholars, politicians and the public is that the Veejack religion pretends not to exist. The Veejack religion does not declare its beliefs publicly. Yet, through its mantra that it "speaks truth," the Veejack religion has been able to insinuate itself and its doctrines into Federal, state, and local governments and the various levels of government. These governments are now compelling participation and adherence to its beliefs at all levels of government including within taxpayer-funded public schools, the provision of public services, and by the imposition of administrative controls on commerce and in other areas.

Most previous disputes about religion in government have involved religions that have declared their religiosity and their dogmas. It is unique in the history of the United States to have a religion like the Veejack faith that refuses to admit to its own existence and thereby is able to insinuate itself relentlessly into the fabric of governmental organizations and the public schools.

When the First Amendment was written the principal disputes about religion were between Protestant sects.[110] As the nation matured the disputes and debates over religion became more diverse. In 1963 Supreme Court Justice Brennan observed that, "today the nation is far more heterogeneous religiously, including as it does substantial minorities not only of Catholics and Jews but as well of those who worship according to no version of the Bible and those who worship no God at all."[111] Justice Brennan is here prophetically describing the Veejack religion, which does not recognize – and in many ways opposes – the teachings in the Bible and does not worship God.

---

[110] Chemerinsky, 1298, quoting Justice Brennan from *Abington School District. V. Schempp*, 374 U.S. 203, 238 (Brennan, J., concurring) (1963).
[111] *Id.*

Another relevant provision of the Constitution that Chemerinsky discusses is Article VI, clause 3, that states "no religious Test shall ever be required as a Qualification to any Office or public Trust under the United States."[112] Sadly, at many levels of government in the United States and in private commercial activity, the Veejack religion's followers have imposed religious tests on employment by selecting for employment those candidates who most vigorously support the tenets of the Veejack faith and excluding those candidates who do not support the Veejack religion. Examples of Veejack religious beliefs that are sought-after in government hiring include covetousness, infanticide, euthanasia, and the theft of wealth from people perceived as "rich" which is then transferred to other people perceived to be "poor".[113] Sadly, even though the Supreme Court has emphatically stated that "neither a State nor the Federal Government can constitutionally force a person to 'profess a belief or disbelief in any religion'"[114] the Veejack religion's members require governmental employees to both profess the Veejack religion's beliefs and deny beliefs, such as within the Judeo-Christian community, that are contrary to the Veejack religion's beliefs.

Unfortunately for those challenging stealth religions such as the Veejack faith, there is little legal clarity in the United States Supreme Court decisions as to what constitutes a religion. The Supreme Court, despite deciding numerous cases about religion, "has avoided trying to formulate a definition" of the word itself.[115] Chemerinsky

---

[112] Chemerinsky, 1298.

[113] There is no definition of either term, and Veejack's leadership uses the terms "rich" and the "poor" as verbal weapons. Veejack condemns the "rich" as brutish oppressors and uplifts the "poor" as revered sufferers. Within the term "rich" Veejack, to suit its propaganda, may include people ranging from hardworking middleclass suburbanites to billionaires. Within the term "poor" Veejack debases its meaning by including those people who are capable of working but choose not to work, such as substance abusers and criminals.

[114] Chemerinsky, 1299, quoting from *Torcaso v. Watkins*, 367 U.S. 488, 495 (1961)

[115] Chemerinsky, 1299. In Thomas v. Review Bd., Ind. Empl. Sec. Div., 450 U.S. 707, 714 (1981) Chief Justice Burger, writing for the Court, noted "(t)he determination of

believes it is "impossible to formulate a definition of religion that encompasses the vast array of spiritual beliefs and practices that are present in the United States."[116]

Again, sadly for those challenging the government's forced participation in stealth religions such as the Veejack faith, the lack of an adequate definition of what constitutes a religion leaves the scholar with only the famous quote from Supreme Court Justice Potter Stewart. Justice Potter, when lacking a definition for hard core pornography stated: "I know it when I see it."[117] And it is clear to all who view the Veejack religion's comprehensive infiltration of government that "they know it when they see it" and they know that the Veejack faith is a religion. Even though the term "religion" has no legal definition, and legally the term "religion" may well be undefinable, the Veejack faith, with it attributes, dictums, tenets and beliefs has no more place in the governmental realm than does the Ten Commandments.

Along with the absence of a definition of the term "religion" from the Supreme Court, "(t)he problem is that the very attempt to define 'religion' is itself misconceived. There simply is no essence of religion, there is no single characteristic or set of characteristics that all religions have in common that makes them religions."[118] And, as with the Veejack religious faith that does not advocate belief in God, to be a religion there is no requirement for a belief in a deity. Analyzing Supreme Court cases as early as 1983, law professor George C. Freeman III wrote:

---

what is a "religious" belief or practice is more often than not a difficult and delicate task."

[116] Chemerinsky, 1299.

[117] Jacobellis v. Ohio, 378 U.S. 184, 197 (Stewart, J., concurring) (1964). Justice Stewart wrote the Court was "faced with the task of trying to define what may be indefinable. * * * I shall not today attempt further to define the kinds of material I understand to be embraced within that shorthand description, and perhaps I could never succeed in intelligibly doing so. But I know it when I see it . . .."

[118] George C. Freeman III, The Misguided Search for the Constitutional Definition of "Religion," 71 Geo. L.J. 1519, 1548 (1983).

Without commenting explicitly in the case on the meaning of "religion," the Court implied that earlier attempts to equate religion with theism were probably unconstitutional. Religious freedom, said the Court, includes "the right to maintain theories of life and of death and of the hereafter which are rank heresy to followers of the orthodox faiths." In 1953, in *Fowler v. Rhode Island*, the Court again suggested that any attempt to reduce religion to theism is constitutionally suspect: "[I]t is no business of courts to say that what is a religious practice or activity for one group is not religion under the protection of the First Amendment.[119]

The Veejack religion, like Buddhism, does not profess to worship a deity or address the issue of whether there is an afterlife. But there is no need to do so. The Veejack religion, with its advocacy of covetousness, infanticide, euthanasia, theft, and other beliefs not traditionally found in religions of peace and love, has no legal requirement to believe in a deity or an afterlife or even the existence of the soul as part of its dogma. Many creeds and belief systems like the Veejack religious faith that pretend to be secular, should nevertheless be identified as a religion under the Constitution.

For example, the teaching of the Science of Creative Intelligence in the propagation of the technique of Transcendental Meditation in a course in the New Jersey public high schools violated the establishment clause of the first amendment.[120] In that case, the Court terminated the teaching of the course as a Constitutionally prohibited establishment of religion.[121] This decision reminds us that notwithstanding the fluid nature of the Veejack religion, which has not yet standardized all of its tenets, beliefs and practices,

---

[119] Freeman III, (internal footnotes deleted).
[120] *Malnak v. Yogi*, 440 F. Supp. 1284 (D.N.J. 1977).
[121] *Malnak v. Yogi*, 440 F. Supp. 1284, 1327 (D.N.J. 1977).

and created numerous sects that encourage vigorous debate and challenges within it practitioners, it is a vital and growing religion.[122] The devotees within the Veejack religion often have conflicted, confused and varying understanding of the Veejack religious teachings.[123] Notwithstanding the multiplicity of doctrinal conflicts within the Veejack religion the Supreme Court has emphatically ruled that "an individual could claim a religious belief even though it was inconsistent with the doctrines of his or her religion."[124] This clearly shows that denials that the Veejack faith is a religion because its doctrines cannot be pinned-down or described with finality are meaningless. Even if there is no comprehensive and universally accepted recitation of the beliefs of the Veejack faith, there are many identifiable beliefs that must be expurgated from the teachings within the public schools, branches of government, and those organizations supported by government funding.

As noted, the United States Constitution's "establishment clause" and the "free exercise clause" are twin protections for the people to exercise freedom of religion. While some scholars have proposed that the definition of "religion" should be different for each of the protections there are no court cases supporting separate definitions.[125] This is because the word "religion" appears only once

---

[122] See, e.g., Marx, Karl and Engels, Friedrich, *On Religion*, Mineola, New York: Dover Publications, Inc., 2008. At 206, Engels writes that "Christianity got hold of the masses, exactly as modern socialism does, under the shape of a variety of sects, and still more conflicting individual views – some clearer, some more confused, these latter the great majority – but all opposed to the ruling system, to the 'powers that be'." As noted elsewhere, Veejack is fairly described as a socialist religion.

[123] At Marx, 330, Engels writes that "mass movements are bound to be confused at the beginning; confused because the thinking of the masses at first moves among contradictions, lack of clarity and lack of cohesion, and also because of the role that prophets play in them at the beginning. * * * So it was with early Christianity, so it was in the beginning of the socialist movement . . . .." The fragmentation of sects within the Veejack religion was thus anticipated by its founders, who cautioned their adherents not to oppose, but to welcome its various sects.

[124] Chemerinsky, 1304, citing *Thomas v. Review Board of the Indiana Employment Security Division*, 450 U.S. 707 (1981).

[125] Chemerinsky, 1300.

in the first amendment.[126] As the word appears only once it should not have multiple and potentially conflicting definitions.

As noted previously, the Supreme Court has never been called on to review a stealth religion that refuses to define itself as a religion. The Supreme Court has only addressed religion in limited circumstances. The Supreme Court has addressed the concept of religion in the context of the Selective Service Act (which established the "drafting" of men into the military), in determine whether a religious belief is sincerely held, and in determining that a sincerely held religious belief is protected by the Constitution "even if it is not the dogma or dominant view within the religion."[127]

The issue of dogma and dominant view within a religion is critical to analyzing the Veejack faith – with its penchant for denying its own existence as a religion – because of the many and divergent sects that are vying for dominance within the Veejack religion itself. Notwithstanding the interreligious battles that are ongoing within the Veejack religion and the fractures and schisms that are waged within the Veejack religion, they must not be accepted by the Courts as an avenue of escape from the protections provided to the people by the First Amendment.

There are three legal theories relating to the first amendment's prohibition on the establishment of religion: strict separation, which holds that to the greatest extent possible government and religion should be separated; the neutrality theory which posits that government must neither favor nor oppose religion over secularism nor one religion over another; and the accommodation

---

[126] *Everson v. Board of Education*, 330 U.S. 1, 32 (Rutledge, J., dissenting) (1947). Justice Rutledge wrote:

"Religion" appears only once in the Amendment. But the word governs two prohibitions, and governs them alike. It does not have two meanings, one narrow, to forbid "an establishment," and another much broader, for securing "the free exercise thereof." "Thereof" brings down "religion" with its entire and exact content, no more and no less, from the first into the second guaranty, so that Congress, and now the states, are as broadly restricted concerning the one as they are regarding the other.

[127] Chemerinsky, 1300.

theory pursuant to which the government should accommodate the presence of religion in government.[128] Of these three theories the most dangerous for protecting the citizenry from the Veejack religion's encroachment and inputting the Veejack religious faith's views into government is the third. The reason is that the government is already, either unknowingly or willfully, accommodating if not proselytizing the Veejack religion's views within its various responsibilities for education, public benefits, and the imposition of administrative controls on commerce, *et cetera*.

The infusion of the beliefs of the Veejack religious faith into the body of political activity within the United States must be stopped, and the VeeJack religion's presence within public education and government must be eliminated completely by enforcing either a strict separation or neutrality. If the Veejack religion's practices are only pruned they would, as happens when a hedge is trimmed, grow back thicker and fuller and obliterate the protections of the First Amendment. Neutrality of the government towards the Veejack religion is only possible after the complete elimination of its practices that have been allowed to permeate and twist the activities of public education, government agencies, and government funding.

The strict separation theory was famously articulated by former President Thomas Jefferson, the drafter of the Declaration of Independence, as building "a wall separating church and state."[129] As argued by law professor Alan Schwarz, however, the doctrine of separation should "prohibit only . . . (activity) which has as its motive or substantial effect the imposition of religious belief or practice . . .."[130] Even by Schwarz' relaxed standard, the Veejack religion's activities and its views on coveting the wealth of others,

---

[128] Chemerinsky, 1305-1311.

[129] Chemerinsky, 1305, quoting Thomas Jefferson, Letters to Messrs. Nehemiah Dodge and others, a Committee of the Danbury Baptist Association, Writings, 510 (1984).

[130] Alan Schwarz, "No Imposition of Religion: The Establishment Clause Value", 77 Yale L.J. 692, 693 (1968).

theft, murder, and its belief that human activity can impact the climate must be prohibited from public education, and other governmental activities.[131]

Separation of religion and government is essential to protecting religious liberty. As famously stated by Professor Chemerinsky, "when religion becomes a part of the government . . . there is inevitable coercion to participate in that faith. Those of different faiths and those who profess no religious beliefs are made to feel excluded and unwelcome when government and religion become intertwined."[132] The intertwining of religion and government, moreover, "is inherently divisive in a country with so many different religions and many people who claim no religion at all."[133] It is indeed ironic that one of the judicially protected groups – those advocates of the Veejack faith who claim they have no religion at all (or masquerade as adhering to an established religion by celebrating its holidays without adhering to its beliefs) – are one of the greatest violators of the right of other people to be protected from infliction of religious beliefs within government.

Former Supreme Court Justice Sandra O'Connor examined the neutrality view of separation of religion from government, writing "the government must not make a person's religious beliefs relevant to his or her standing in the political community by conveying a message 'that religion or a particular religious belief is favored or preferred' . . . ."[134] The adherents to the Veejack religion demand of the people adherence to its beliefs on climate, covetousness, theft and murder in educational settings, administrative offices, public benefits and other areas of government. This, as Justice O'Connor

---

[131] Human activity, of course, may impact local air and water purity. See, infra, Chapter Seven "Climate and the Weather Gods."

[132] Chemerinsky, 1305.

[133] Chemerinsky, 1306, citing Marsh v. Chamber, 463 U.S. 783 (1983) (Brennan, J., dissenting).

[134] *County of Allegheny v. American Civil Liberties Union, Greater Pittsburgh Chapter*, 492 U.S. 573, 627 (1989) (O'Connor, J., concurring in part and concurring in the judgment) (internal citations omitted).

observed, sends to the people of Abrahamic and other religions that differ from the Veejack faith, "a clear message . that they . . . are outsiders or less than full members of the . . . community."[135]

There are egregious examples of the Veejack religion advocating its religious views in public displays in public schools, government administrative buildings and other venues. The displays advocate the Veejack religion's views on adherence to weather and climate doctrine, coveting the wealth of working Americans, "historical" descriptions that are inaccurate and misleading to convey a message supporting the Veejack religion's doctrines. Such displays, in the view of Supreme Court Justices Stevens and Ginsburg create "symbolic endorsement . . . if a reasonable person passing by would perceive government support for religion."[136] Justice Stevens wrote "(i)f a reasonable person could perceive a government endorsement of religion from a private display, then the State may not allow its property to be used as a forum for that display. No less stringent rule can adequately protect nonadherents from a well-grounded perception that their sovereign supports a faith to which they do not subscribe."[137]

As Professor Chemerinsky writes, a "key purpose of the establishment clause is to prevent the government from making those who are not a part of the favored religion feel unwelcome."[138] The Veejack religion's use of public spaces to convey its religious views not only makes a nonadherent feel unwelcome, the nonadherent is ostracized, mocked and worse. As Supreme Court Justice Blackmun wrote, "it is not enough that the government restrain from compelling religious practices: It must not engage in them either."[139]

---

[135] *Id.*

[136] Chemerinsky, 1308.

[137] *Capitol Square Review and Advisory Board v. Pinette*, 515 U.S. 753, 799-800 (1995) (Stevens, J., dissenting).

[138] Chemerinsky, 1308.

[139] Lee v. Weisman, 505 U.S. 577, 604 (1992) (Blackmun, J., concurring).

CHAPTER THREE

MARX AND ENGELS ORIGINATE THE VEEJACK RELIGION

Most students of Marxism, socialism, and communism are firm in their belief that Karl Marx and Friedrich Engels, the founders of modern socialism, were opposed to religion. However, in the book *On Religion*,[140] which contains the writings most associated with the hypothesis that Marx and Engels were opposed to religion, they set forth many of the tenets of the socialistic Veejack religious faith. This chapter will explain Marx's and Engel's concepts that underlie the dogma and beliefs of the Veejack religion.[141]

---

[140] Marx. While *On Religion* contains essays by both Marx and Engels references to "*On Religion*" or "Marx" will be used to refer to quoted material, with the appropriate page number. Please note that for purposes of this analysis the text as translated for Dover Publications will be faithfully followed. However, the word "man" should be understood as including all "humankind." Marx and Engels wrote during a period of male chauvinism and their language reflects the cultural norms of the late 19th century.

[141] See, e.g., Gutierrez, Gustavo, *A Theology of Liberation – 15th Anniversary Edition*, Maryknoll, New York: Orbis Books 2021. Here, Gutierrez edges very close to recognizing socialism as a religion. Gutierrez writes that "Marxist thought (is) focusing on praxis and geared to the transformation of the world. * * * Many agree with Sartre that 'Marxism, (is) the formal framework of all contemporary philosophical thought'.

Europe in the late 17th and 18th centuries was an intellectually exciting period as movements, such as the "Enlightenment",[142] emphasized reason and individualism rather than tradition. Philosophers such as René Descartes, John Locke, and Isaac Newton, joined by Immanuel Kant, Johann Wolfgang von Goethe, François-Marie Arouet (more commonly known by his *nom de plume* M. de Voltaire), Jean-Jacques Rousseau, and others championed these values. This era spawned post-theologians such as Marx and Engels who propounded theories of secular culture, who took advantage of antireligious sentiments and exposed the fragile nature of "modern rational consciousness."[143] This fragility of the rational consciousness fostered "unconscious systemic distortions" in individual lives and within society as whole.[144] Marx and Engels, themselves suffering from unconscious societal distortions about religion and reality, then criticized existing religions without recognizing that they were simultaneously creating a new religion: an essentially socialist religion now known as the Veejack religion.

As observed in the previous paragraph, the followers of the socialist Veejack religion, endorsed strongly by their admirers in the academic community and media, would applaud the statement on the rear cover of *On Religion* where Marx "declared religion the opiate of the people . . .."[145] The statement on the rear cover of *On*

---

* * * (And) contemporary theology does in fact find itself in direct . . . confrontation with Marxism . . ..", at 9. Sadly, socialism's adherence to atheism rejects otherworldly salvation in any religion according to Gutierrez, because socialism is focused on "the value of earthly existence", 85.

[142] The Age of the Enlightenment, which is often referred to as the "Age of Reason", occurred in Europe in 17th and 18th centuries. It focused on human happiness, accruing knowledge using reason and sensory evidence, and encouraged ideas and ideals, especially the separation of church and state.

[143] Tracy, David, *Plurality and Ambiguity*, San Francisco: Harper & Row, 1987, 76.

[144] Tracy, 76.

[145] Marx at 42, "religion is the sigh of the oppressed . . . (and) the heart of a heartless world" and "the opium of the people."

Religion continues that the writings in the book "constitute(s) the theoretical basis of proletarian Marxist atheism."[146]

Unlike Buddhism, Jainism, Confucianism, and non-theist Quakers, which admit their status as atheistic religions, the socialist Veejack religion does not admit – nor do many of its practitioners know – that it is a religion and, instead, pretends to be merely a political or economic philosophy. However, as will be demonstrated below, the socialist Veejack religion is an atheistic faith.[147] It must be emphasized that as an atheistic religious faith, the Veejack faith is entitled to all of the protections provided by the Constitution and the Veejack religion's believers safeguarded in their beliefs; however, as with religions who admit their existence and do not hide behind a veil of secrecy and obfuscation, the Veejack religion must be restrained from entering and proselytizing it views and beliefs within governmental organizations, public schools, and administrative offices.[148]

Marx believed that atheism was the best belief.[149] And that a society of atheists was possible.[150] Further, Marx argued that it is

---

[146] Marx, rear cover of book.

[147] That the socialist Veejack religion exists is not a new or unique idea. As early as the 1840s the religion of socialism was identified publicly. The expression "*donc, lathéisme c'est votre religion*", or "atheism is your religion" was so prevalent that Engels, at 239, felt obligated to deny its validity. Unfortunately for the United States, the repeated denials of the adherents of the socialist religion – now known as Veejack – that it is a religion linger to this day. The denials that Veejack is a religion have insulated and allowed Veejack to permeate governmental administrative and educational institutions to the detriment of both the United States Constitution and other religions.

[148] To paraphrase and reverse the statement of German philosopher Ludwig von Feuerbach, who said, "politics must become our religion," Marx and Engels successors have created the socialist Veejack religion as their politics. See, Marx, 242.

[149] Hoffer, at 86, acknowledged that "(t)he atheist is a religious person . . . (and) believes in atheism as though it were a new religion . . . (and) is an atheist with devoutness and unction."

[150] See, also, at 142, Engels' observation that "it is easy . . . to be an atheist." Engels, at 143, further asserts that "atheism . . . (should be) a compulsory article of faith . . . (and laws should be enacted) prohibiting religion generally." Engels, at 151, observes that

"not by atheism, but by superstition and idolatry that man debases himself."[151] It cannot be gainsaid, but that Marx is here criticizing theistic theology, especially the Abrahamic religions.[152] Marx was especially caustic in his references to God. Marx wrote, "since only what is material is perceptible, knowable, nothing is known of the existence of God."[153] Marx, in an essay cowritten by Engels, caustically observed that "the kingdom of God . . . (never) existed anywhere except in the imagination . . .."[154] Engels, too, denied that God was active in the creation of humankind. Engels wrote that "man is the sole animal capable of working his way out of the merely animal state – his normal state is one appropriate to his consciousness, one that has to be created by himself."[155]

Engels slyly attacked religions while formulating at the same time the tenets of the socialist religion that evolved into the modern Veejackian faith. Engels, persuading his followers that the religion of socialism, the modern Veejack religion, was merely an ideology, wrote that "every ideology . . . once it has arisen, develops in connection with the given concept-material, and develops this material further; otherwise it would not be an ideology . . . with thoughts as with

---

"only real knowledge of the forces of nature ejects the gods or God from one position after another." Surprisingly, the socialist Veejack religion has abandoned this position in favor of believing that humankind, in its actions or inactions, holds sway over the forces of nature. This is evident in Veejack's adoption of the belief that humankind impacts weather, climate, and other forces of nature. The belief that humankind through its conduct influences nature harkens back to the earliest cultic beliefs that obeisance must be paid to the gods of nature, or they would inflict upon them storms, tornados, floods, drought, or other natural horrors. Thus, in contradistinction to Engels, Veejack demands that its adherents forfeit comfort and cash to the gods of weather and climate through restrictions on indoor temperature control and taxes on the use of fuel and power.

[151] Marx, 63.

[152] Engels, likewise, at 120, criticizes Mohammed's religion. Editor's Note: Mohammed founded the religion of Islam.

[153] Marx, 65.

[154] Marx, 80.

[155] Marx, 192.

independent entities, developing independently and subject only to their own laws."[156]

Engels, trying to obscure his development of the religion of socialism (i.e., the Veejack religion) and maintain the falsehood that he was opposed to all religion was particularly critical of both Christianity and Islam.[157] Engels refers to Christianity as "nonsense"[158] and asserts that Islam could not achieve success in the West.[159] As to God and angels, Engels wrote that "nothing exists outside nature and man, and the higher beings our religious fantasies have created are only the fantastic reflection of our own essence."[160] Prematurely insinuating the demise of Christianity, Engels wrote that Christianity has "entered into its final stage . . (and has) become incapable for the future of serving any progressive class as the ideological garb of its aspirations."[161] More than a century after these words were written the Christian church, while under attack by the Veejack religion's adherents in the United States, is growing worldwide and flourishing.

Marx's attacks on theistic religious belief are anathema to the principles of American separation of church and state. This is especially applicable to public educational institutions. Within the United States Marx's teachings are openly read and taught to young students. This elevation of Marx's teachings above other religious teachings is unconstitutional. The dialogues of Marx, and other Veejack religious theologians, should be on the same footing as the Bible, Quran and other religious texts and allowed into public education curriculum only in specific and fully explained circumstances. Marx's writings should not be taught as "truth" but should be labeled and identified as religious texts.

---

[156] Marx, 263.
[157] At Marx, 194-204, Engels' essay *Bruno Bauer and Early Christianity* severely criticizes both Christianity and Islam.
[158] Marx, 195.
[159] Marx, 203.
[160] Marx, 224.
[161] Marx, 266.

Marx opens with the dictum that "the consciousness of man . . . (is) the supreme divinity. There must be no god on a level with it."[162] Marx here succinctly summarizes the underlying belief of the socialist Veejack religion: that the ever-changing and mutating thoughts of the Veejack religion's spokespeople – in essence what its adherents believe at any given time – are supreme, divine and must be followed.[163] Orwell, in his novel *1984*, portrays its fictional fascistic government as also adopting the practice of imposing a constantly changing message on the people. Marx advocates for the amorphous "general rights of society" as the goal and urges that "only in the name of the general rights of society can a particular class vindicate for itself general domination."[164] Engels echoes Marx's belief that society is delineated into classes of people, writing, ". . . all political struggles are class struggles, and all class struggles for emancipation . . . for every class struggle is a political struggle (and) turn ultimately on the question of economic emancipation."[165]

The belief within the Veejack religion that society is divided into immutable classes has spawned more hatred, suffering and misery than almost any other tenet of the socialist Veejack religion. Although in the United States people of all sexes, races, ethnicities, and nationalities continue to rise to the highest level of business, politics, and the arts and achieve enormous economic success, the myth that people are born into, and remain, members of a particular class is still a firm tenet of the socialist Veejack religion. There are

---

[162] Marx, at 15.

[163] Marx opens the door here to sloganeering and to the inconsistent application of his beliefs by teaching, at 50, that "man is the highest essence for man, hence with the categoric imperative to overthrow all relations in which man is debased, enslaved, abandoned . . . (and despised)." While appearing impressive, this language offers no guideposts and instead encourages people to act on their personal desires. This underlies the Veejack toleration of theft, riot, arson, and other criminal activity as tools for righting perceived wrongs. Too often, the perception of a "wrong" is transitory, subject to change, and based on an individual's personal view.

[164] Marx, 54.

[165] Marx, 259.

numerous examples of racial, religious, and ethnic minority people's success stories and their economic upward mobility via hard work, education, and perseverance. However, the Veejack faith's adherents continue to communicate undefined and ephemeral concepts of people being locked into the economic status in which they are born. The Veejack religion raises the concept of class bondage as a sacred myth to advocate for civil unrest, theft, "flash mob" robbery, mayhem, arson, and destruction.

This differs substantially from other religions that have prescribed catechism and basic philosophical, ethical, and moral beliefs. Marx urges the elimination of other religions, arguing "the abolition of religion as the illusory happiness of the people is required for their real happiness."[166] This startlingly intolerant viewpoint underlies much of the Veejack religion's philosophy of recruiting adherents by denouncing other religions. It also underlies the Veejack religion's intense opposition to the Judeo-Christian religions.

Marx believed that historical cultures and civilizations had unique religions and, at times, even "art and rhetoric has superseded religion."[167] Marx considered religious belief to be a flexible concept, noting that when a civilization collapsed it was common for the civilization's religion to collapse as well.[168] In short, Marx believed that "man makes religion, religion does not make man."[169]

Marx believed that the religions of the Greco-Roman world "perished because scientific research disclosed the errors of the antique religions."[170] Marx's belief in the ultimate power of scientific research

---

[166] Marx, 42.

[167] Marx, 23.

[168] Marx, at 23, observes that "it was not the downfall of the old religions that brought the downfall of the old states, but the downfall of the old states that brought the downfall of the old religions."

[169] Marx, 41. And Marx helped create Veejack as a religion.

[170] Marx, 23. Many Greco-Roman holidays survived the collapse of the Roman Empire. And many Greco-Roman gods remain today as literary figures or comic book heroes such as Aphrodite, Ares, Bacchus, Eros, Hermes, Pan, Poseidon, and Zeus. See, e.g., https://www2.classics.upenn.edu/myth/php/homer/index.php?page=gods

is now a fundamental principle of the Veejack religion. It is most recently reflected in the Veejack faith's veneration of climatologists, who apocalyptically predict the end of the known world unless the Veejack religion's (often changing) edicts are zealously followed. That science is greater than Abrahamic religion is firmly embedded in the Veejack religion's belief systems; and the belief that science is greater than Abrahamic religion can be directly traced, as noted above, to the writings of Marx.

Along with adulating science, Marx advocates the concept of human reason as a religious ikon. Marx believes that worldly and religious reason contradict each other.[171] Marx's Veejack religious belief stresses the ascendancy of science over religion as a key tenet of the Veejack religion.[172] Marx also argues that philosophy's metaphysical truths "do not know the boundaries of political geography," [173] thus introducing the Veejack faith's denunciation of national boundaries which is exemplified in the porous border enforcement and unchecked illegal immigration into the United States beginning in 2021.

Marx's belief in the supremacy of the human mind over what he called "the illusory horizon of particular world and national outlooks"[174] reinforces the key tenet of the socialist Veejack religion that contemporary – and perhaps fleeting – human thought is more important than the laws and customs of individual nations. The Veejack religion, as noted, keenly enforces this belief by arguing for unrestricted migration, open national borders, and within the United States the abandonment of Federalism and the imposition

---

[171] Marx, 24.

[172] In order, however, for Veejack to bend and mutate its belief as the need arises, Engels, at Marx, 284, propounded the theory that "science" is ever-changing. Engels wrote that "the history of science is the history of gradually clearing away . . . nonsense or rather of its replacement by fresh but always less absurd nonsense." By both championing science while simultaneously admitting that science is ever-changing Veejack sees no inconsistency in constantly reversing course.

[173] Marx, 26.

[174] Marx, 26.

of a national legal system rather than maintaining the Federalist concept of each constituent state maintaining its own legal system.

Marx believed that the "living soul of culture" is transitory and spawns only a philosophy that is the "spiritual quintessence of its time."[175] In other words, it is appropriate for the Veejack religion to evolve and modify its beliefs and ideas as the times change. This acceptance by its leaders of a transitory belief system shifts power and authority to the current leaders of the Veejack religion. It also limits the Veejack religion's members' ability to challenge the constantly changing views of the Veejack religion's leaders because there is no permanent ideological scaffolding sustaining the Veejack religion beyond the supremacy of science and human thought. Marx wrote that "the people must be taught to be terrified at itself in order to give it courage."[176] This advocacy of self-hate is diametrically opposed to the Abrahamic traditions of peaceful coexistence and love.

Another totem[177] strongly advocated by the Veejack religion is the glorification of "truth."[178] Marx leaves to academic historians to ascertain the extent of truth, writing, "the task of history . . . is to establish the truth of this world."[179] Even though what constitutes "truth" is whatever the leaders of the Veejack religion say it is at any given time, Marx castigates other religions because they "promise

---

[175] Marx, 31.

[176] Marx, 45. Please note that while Marx addressed these words to the people of Germany, like St Paul in his letters to discrete congregations that are respected by the Christian church at large, the religion of socialism/Veejack reads Marx's words and teachings as applying to all people at all times.

[177] Durant, Will, *Our Oriental Heritage*, New York: MJF Books, 1935, renewed 1963, 61-62, explains "the Ojibwa Indians gave the name *totem* to their special sacred animal . . . and this confused word has stumbled into anthropology as *totemism*, denoting vaguely any worship of a particular object . . . (or belief) as particularly sacred to the group."

[178] In fact, most of Veejack's teachings on climate, language and pronouns, race, ethnicity, gender fluidity, and religion itself are bound up in the amorphous illogical underpinning that their teachings are true because they are true. This absurd tautology is the heart of the Veejack faith.

[179] Marx, 42.

heaven and earth, . . . (while the religion of socialism/Veejack) promises nothing but the truth."[180] As Marx phrased it, "any state which is not the embodiment of rational freedom is a bad state."[181] Again, Marx opens the door to constantly changing views within the Veejack religion because the concept of "rational freedom" is too ephemeral and illusory to harness and rein in the views of the Veejack religion's leaders. With the Veejack religion arguing for "truth" and rational freedom as guideposts, its moral and philosophical directional signs can swing wildly like a weathervane in a storm at a moment's notice.

Engels, a founding architect of the Veejack religious faith, had an elastic conception of the concept of "truth." Engels taught that all stages of human society are transient.[182] Each human stage, he believed, gradually loses its validity and justification, and gives way to another human stage that will, as well, decay and perish. As Engels describes it, "truth" is transitory. Engels wrote, that "just as the bourgeoisie by large-scale industry, competition, and the world market dissolves in practice all stable time-honored institutions, so this dialectical philosophy dissolves all conceptions of final, absolute truth . . . ."[183]

Having in theory demolished the concept of "absolute truth," Marx and Engels then postulated the elasticity and transitory aspect of any given "truth". This hypothesis then opened the door to the Veejack religion's dialectical substitution, and succession, of one truth for another; and given the appropriate circumstances, the resuscitation of discarded truths.[184]

Marx is superficially critical of industry and wealth, at times

---

[180] Marx, 33.

[181] Marx, 38.

[182] Marx, 218.

[183] Marx, 218.

[184] For the members of the Veejack religion the revolving nature of "truths" is most profound in Veejack's injection of itself into politics. When the Veejack religion's favored political party is in power the "truths" that were used to challenge the opposing political party are often discarded – even denied – as ideas discarded are resurrected;

arguing that industry and wealth are major problems.[185] However, Marx spreads confusion among his followers by advocating the dichotomy of using the weapon of material force to overthrow materialism.[186] As Marx, again using vague and undefined polemical language to urge his followers to violence, writes:

> Only in the name of the general rights of society can a particular class vindicate for itself general domination. For the storming of this emancipatory position, and hence for the political exploitation of all sections of society in the interests of its own section, revolutionary energy and spiritual self-feeling alone are not sufficient. For the revolution of a nation and the emancipation of a particular class of civil society to coincide . . . all the defects of society must conversely be concentrated in another class . . . so that liberation from (notorious social crime) . . . appears as general self-liberation.[187]

With these words Marx opens the door for the Veejack religion to determine on its own which people are authorized to articulate grievances, and against which other people those grievances are to be directed.[188] The undefined concepts of people inhabiting classes that have unique interests and require emancipation through self-help

---

and previously propounded truths discarded. This often leaves the Veejack members unable to develop critical thinking skills.

[185] See, e.g., Marx at 46, writing "the relation of industry, of the world of wealth generally, to the political world is one of the major problems of modern times."

[186] Marx, 50.

[187] Marx, 54.

[188] The airing of grievances, in a bizarre "art imitating life", was popularly satirized as the holiday "Festivus" in the 1990s television show *Seinfeld*. As described by Wikipedia, the non-commercial holiday's celebration, as depicted on *Seinfeld*, occurs on December 23 and includes a Festivus dinner, an unadorned aluminum Festivus pole, and practices such as the "airing of grievances". Available at https://en.wikipedia.org/wiki/Festivus

based on "feelings" is rife within the senior leadership of the Veejack religion. This language is interpreted by the leaders of the Veejack religion[189] as authorizing indiscriminate violence, theft, arson, assault, and riot based on perceptions, whims, and selfish desires. Marx further muddies the waters by claiming that even when there is no discernible wrong being committed, "universal suffering . . . (may be blamed) on wrong generally" and justify violent action.[190] And the violence Marx sanctions need not be instigated to achieve a specific goal other than causing strife. Engels championed the concept of picking fights knowing his side would lose, because as he saw it, "in the long run the vanquished often gains more economically, politically and morally than the victor."[191] Sadly, some adherents of the Veejack religion while caught up in the frenzy of the moment willingly impale themselves on the spear of futile endeavor in the mistaken belief that losing is winning, and their sacrifice is somehow advancing their Veejack religious commitment.[192] Despite subscribing to an atheistic religion with no concept of an afterlife the deluded victims of this deception cling to the belief that their suffering is worthwhile.[193] The adherents engaging in this self-destructive and futile anarchistic action do not stop to think that the elites of the Veejack religion, who live in gated estates and travel

---

[189] It is important to note that many of Veejack's leaders pretend to be members of other faiths. Some Veejack leaders, for example, while ignoring Catholic teachings and/or Papal Encyclicals, still claim to be devout Catholics.

[190] Marx, 56-57.

[191] Marx, 282.

[192] Examples of Veejack believers willingly giving themselves up to harm or arrest occur in almost every Veejack-inspired march, protest, or demonstration. Veejack tactics include inviting photo and print journalists to broadcast these antics because they hope to achieve Engels' prediction that "the vanquished . . . (will gain more) economically, politically and morally than the victor."

[193] Engels succinctly stated this tenet of the religion of socialism (Marx, 316). Noting that "both Christianity and the workers' (Veejack religion of) socialism preach forthcoming salvation from bondage and misery; Christianity places this salvation in a life beyond, after death, in heaven; (the Veejack religion of) socialism places it in this world, in a transformation of society."

with security forces to protect them from harm, could care less that the person committing the futile act may spend months or years in prison. In this regard, Engels championed the faithful of the Veejack religion "to be zealous in propaganda, to courageous and proud confession of their faith in face of the foe, to unrelenting struggle against the enemy both within and without . . .."[194]

Here emerges another of the tenets of the Veejack religion: the end of private property.[195] Marx advocated his followers demand "the negation of private property"[196] and this position has been adopted by the Veejack religion. However, it must be observed that the leaders of the Veejack religion do not believe that it applies to their own property because they are pure and know the "truth"; but the private property of non-adherents is open to appropriation through self-help by those who consider themselves oppressed or by onerous governmental taxation. In this way, the riotous behavior and theft of private property is routinely justified by the leadership of the Veejack religious faith.

Marx's writings are also the seed that gave rise to the Veejack religion's invasive societal weed of defunding the police. Regarding criminals and crime, Marx wrote that "crime must not be punished in the individual, but the anti-social source of crime must be destroyed, and each man must be given social scope for the vital manifestation of his being."[197]

With the maxim "crime must not be punished in the individual" ringing in their ears and echoed in their literature and speeches, the Veejack religion turns the criminal justice system on its head. These words are the basis of the singularly idiotic tenet of the Veejack religion that criminals are not responsible for their reprehensible conduct. Instead, the Veejack religion believes that society is responsible for individual criminal behavior. This bunkum is behind the Veejack

---

[194] Marx, 333-334.
[195] Marx, 57.
[196] Marx, 57.
[197] Marx, 67-68.

religion's advocating for no-bail release of suspects, minimal or no prison time for convicted criminals, and the abolition of the death penalty for even the most depraved and vicious torturers and killers.

Marx is well known as the author of the *Manifesto of the Communist Party*, which is one of the key repositories of the doctrines of the Veejack religion. Even the name of this document is inapt. It would more properly be named the *Manifesto of the Veejack Religion*. For the Veejack religion's doctrine of "truth," Marx writes that there are "eternal truths, such as freedom, justice, etc., that are common to all states of society. But communism[198] abolishes eternal truths, it abolishes all religion, and all morality, instead of constituting them on a new basis; it therefore acts in contradiction to all past historical experience."[199] This is surprisingly inconsistent with Marx's earlier observations (quoted above) that his views, now incorporated into the general doctrines of the Veejack religion, promised "nothing but the truth."[200] However, it is consistent with the tenet of the Veejack religion that "truth" is malleable and means, at any given time and place and no matter how inconsistent with previous statements, whatever the leaders of the Veejack religion say it means.[201]

---

[198] E.g., In the United States it is the Veejack religion.

[199] Marx, 89. This passage is from extracts of the *Manifesto of the Communist Party* that are included in *On Religion*. The cited page numbers refer to *On Religion*.

[200] See, reference above, to the quoted language from Marx, at page 33.

[201] Veejack's beliefs also hold that the definitions of words and concepts are malleable. That the meanings of speeches and writing, even if they occurred long in the past, may be changed to disparage the authors by redefining their words to completely change their meaning. The horrors of societies that adopt Veejack's dystopian model are chronicled in George Orwel's novels *Animal Farm* and *1984*.

CHAPTER FOUR

THE VEEJACK RELIGION AND WHY IT REFUSES TO IDENTIFY ITSELF

A significant aspect of religious activity is to teach life and lifestyle behavior to the religion's young adherents and provide wisdom to its adults. For the Judeo-Christian faiths the biblical books of Proverbs, Ecclesiastes, Song of Songs, Wisdom, Sirach, and the teachings of the prophets and Jesus fulfill this function. Buddhism, Hinduism, Islam, Confucianism, and Dao have similar writings that teach the young and inspire prudence and insight in adults. The Judeo-Christian faiths, Buddhism, Hinduism, Islam, Confucianism, and Dao teach self-discipline, practicality, judgement, initiative, and discretion.

The Veejack religion derives its impetus from socialism in the writings of Marx, Engels, and other writers, including Michael Harrington in the United States. These authors are the sources of wisdom for the atheist Veejack religion.[202] The Veejack religion encourages a belief in individual and collective victimhood. It teaches

---

[202] Marx, at 41, emphasizes that "man makes religion, religion does not make man." Although his language is androcentric, Marx correctly predicts the origin of the Veejack religion that emerged from his and other socialist writings.

individuals they have no chance to succeed because of so-called "systemic" factors that are designed to keep them in subservient roles. Another tenet, specific to the Veejack religious elites is that they do not trust ordinary people and seek to control and dominate them.

The history of the Veejack religion in the United States has been a taboo subject for historians, academics, broadcast and print media, and other researchers because of its virulent and violent tendencies and vigorous attacks on those who dare to challenge its protected position in American society. The Veejack religion intimidates practitioners of other religions and didactically imposes its beliefs, styled as "truth" on public educational institutions, academia, and governmental organizations.

The Veejack faith began to emerge as a religion in the 19th century during the decline of monarchies and empires. As with all "rising religious movements" as Eric Hoffer has observed, "it was all change and experiment – open to new views and techniques from all quarters."[203] It grew in appeal during the chaos following World War I and expanded its adherents during the depression of the 1930s. Following the post-World War II baby-boom and growth of suburban living, the Veejack religion in the United States arrived in full bloom in the uneven prosperity of the 21st century as a new non-theistic religion. Following the path of previous new religions the Veejack faith sought its followers in the disaffected. As Hoffer noted, ". . . the disaffected are found in all walks of life, they are most frequent in the following categories: (a) the poor, (b) misfits, (c) outcasts, (d) minorities, (e) adolescent youth, (f) the ambitious . . . (g) those in the grip of some vice or obsession, (h) the impotent . . . (i) the inordinately selfish, (j) the bored, [and] (k) the sinners."[204]

The Veejack religion, unlike previous religious movements that sought to expand membership by erecting structures and

---

[203] Hoffer, at 4.
[204] Hoffer, 25.

publicly confessing its views, adopted a stealth approach. One of the key reasons for this approach was the unique provision of the United States Constitution, in the First Amendment, that states that "Congress shall make no law respecting an establishment of religion . . . ."[205] This provision has been expanded to prohibit religions from public governmental organizations, such as schools, and governmental executive departments, or to receive governmental funding.[206]

By adopting a stealth approach to its existence and refusing to identify itself as a religion the Veejack faith has been largely successful in inserting its views into public schools, governmental departments, and public funding.[207] Disguising its views as "truth", the Veejack religion manipulates its adherents into obedience. Surprisingly, many of its most steadfast adherents do not recognize that they have been converted to the Veejack religious faith. They believe they either have no religious affiliation or are members of a recognized sect otherwise prevalent in the United States to which they had previously owed allegiance. One of the reasons this is possible is that the Veejack faith permits its adherents to adopt the surface attributes of, and to continue to express loyalty to, other religions. The key dynamic for the Veejack religion is

---

[205] U.S. Const, Amend 1.

[206] See, e.g., *Everson v. Board of Education*, 330 U.S. 1 (1947). See, also, Chapter Two "First Amendment Guarantees and Protections".

[207] Exacerbating public school students' feelings of impotence and powerlessness is Veejack's sinister practice of inducing within the public schools the pernicious doctrine of grade leveling. The Veejack mantra for public educators is that "all students are winners" regardless of whether they have even rudimentary capabilities in reading, writing, math, science, or keyboarding. This doctrine is propounded by Veejack-inspired teachers and is heard in public schools across the nation. The failure of the public schools to enforce universal attendance is tragic. Equally tragic is the teachers' failure to demand accountability in students. Veejack public education policy precludes teachers from explaining to the students that academic achievement requires dedication, hard work, self-discipline, sacrifice and time management; and the absence of rewards for excellence and sanctions and disapproval for substandard performance are all factors in the ethos of the Veejack religion.

that its followers must always adhere to Veejack's core beliefs and respect the decisions of the Veejack religion's leadership.[208] One of its religious characteristics is that the Veejack faith absolutely prohibits compromise on key issues and enforces its will using humiliation, shunning, and violence. As the Veejack religion does not utilize traditional structures, such as cathedrals, churches, synagogues, or mosques to proselytize its message and directives the Veejack religious faith transmits it doctrinal messaging using public school and other educators, politicians, columnists, radio and TV hosts, comedy clubs and both print and electronic media influencers.[209]

The Veejack religion, as noted previously, is characterized by views inconsistent with, and even challenging, Judeo-Christian theology.[210] As an example, the Judeo-Christian religion teaches

---

[208] Veejack adopted the fanaticism described in Orwell's *1984*, at 250, that "The Party seeks power entirely for its own sake. (It is) . . . not interested in the good of others; (it is) . . . interested solely in power. Not wealth or luxury or long life or happiness: only power, pure power."

[209] Veejack employs many diverse strategies to ensure election of its supporters. Veejack's goal is to foster a disinterested and uniformed electorate. For example, Veejack discourages one-day/same-day voting and encourages drawn-out elections. Veejack knows that when voters all cast their ballots on the same day the process and accompanying publicity creates within the people a mutually reinforcing interest and desire to become educated on the issues. The one-day voting process enables the community to form a consensus on what the issues are, and which candidates supports their view of the issues. Veejack knows the psychology of scheduling and, under the guise of encouraging greater voter participation, manipulates the electorate not to vote. Veejack knows that when there is one specific day set aside for voting busy citizens will "build" that day into their calendars to ensure they participate. However, when voting is spread out over many weeks the busy people will delay participation and eventually forget to vote. Allowing continuous drip-drip voting by mail or other drop-by tactics detracts from the importance of the voting process and tends to limit voting to activists who generate attendance by the poor and wealthy leisure classes. The leisure-poor are intimidated into accepting rides to the polls and then told how to vote. The wealthy Veejack elites can manipulate their schedules or have their servants obtain mail-in ballots for them.

[210] Veejack, and its allies in the Jewish and Christian faiths, portray Jesus as an illiterate wanderer, and a budding socialist. Jesus was highly literate, and he was not

that there are two genders: male and female.[211] The Veejack faith, as with many religions from antiquity, advances the theory that there are multiple genders, and that an individual born as male, or female may switch gender. The view that an individual may switch gender, referred to as "transgender", is endorsed by the American Psychological Association.[212]

Society must not restrict or punish the adherents to, or practitioners of, bisexual or multiple gender theory. People of bisexual or transgender orientation must be recognized as legitimate by society, but it must be recognized that these practices represent a religious belief and not a "truth" to be imposed on persons of other religious beliefs via public education, executive or legislative action, or other public funding. The religious nature of bisexual and transgender relationships is described in many places. For example, the Catholic church recently issued a declaration.

> The declaration, called "Infinite Dignity," was approved by Pope Francis and said that God created men and women as biologically different beings, and that no one should try to alter that plan or "make oneself God." The document describes gender-affirming surgery as violating God's

---

a socialist. Jesus was a rabbi and was extremely well read. Jesus was an expert in the Torah, the writings of the Prophets, and Jewish history and teachings. Jesus taught from the Jewish writings, or what Christians refer to as the Old Testament. Jesus' views, values, and relationship with God were Jewish theology. See, e.g., John 8:1-8. None of the books of the New Testament existed when Jesus walked the earth. All of the books that became the New Testament, and the values embraced in them, were based on Jewish theology. Veejack has a goal of denigrating and degrading Judeo-Christian theology, culture, values and disrespecting each individual's relationship with God.

[211] See, e.g., Genesis 1:27 "God created mankind in his image, in the image of God he created them, male and female he created them."

[212] See, e.g., Glicksman, Eve, "Transgender Today - Throughout history, transgender people have been misunderstood and seldom studied. That's beginning to change," Vol 44, No. 4, April 2013, at https://www.apa.org/monitor/2013/04/transgender

gift of human dignity and as attempting to play God on the surgeon's table during a "sex-change intervention."[213]

Prominent historian Will Durant, in his classic "The Story of Civilization", explains that Mesopotamian goddess Ishtar "was the goddess of war as well as of love, of prostitutes as well as of mothers; she called herself 'a compassionate courtesan'; she was represented sometimes as a bearded bisexual deity . . .."[214] Other writers have been more specific, with Allen Mercedes writing that:

> In the Middle East . . . MTF (male-to-female) priestesses were known to have served Astarte, Dea Syria, Atargatis and Ashtoreth / Ishtar. Additional MTF "gallae" served Cybele, the Phrygians' embodiment of The Great Mother. * * * In Africa, intersexed deities and spiritual beliefs in gender transformation are recorded in Akan, Ambo-Kwanyama, Bobo, Chokwe, Dahomean (Benin), Dogon, Bambara, Etik, Handa, Humbe, Hunde, Ibo, Jukun, Kimbundu, Konso, Kunama, Lamba, Lango, Luba, Lugbara (where MTFs are called okule and FTMs are called agule), Lulua, Musho, Nat, Nuba, Ovimbundu, Rundi, Sakpota,

---

[213] Dorgan, Michael, "Catholic monk comes out as transgender with diocese's permission", May 23, 2024, Fox News at https://www.foxnews.com/us/catholic-monk-comes-out-transgender-diocese-permission. The Judeo-Christian faiths are struggling with the transsexual possibilities that modern medical surgical procedures have introduced. Although the Catholic message in "Infinite Dignity" is opposed to transexual surgical procedures, a transexual Catholic monk is serving as a hermit in the Dioceses of Lexington, Kentucky. As Bishop John Stowe of the Diocese observed, "'Hermits are a rarely used form of religious life ... but they can be either male or female,' Stowe said. 'Because there's no pursuit of priesthood or engagement in sacramental ministry, and because the hermit is a relatively quiet and secluded type of vocation, I didn't see any harm in letting him live this vocation'".

[214] Durant, 235.

Shona-Karonga, Venda, Vili-Kongo, and Zulu tribes. * * * (In India many) worshipped the mother-goddess Bahuchara Mata, although some also worshipped Shiva in his half-man, half-woman persona, Ardhanarisvara. Many early Indonesian societies had transgender figures in religious functions, including the basaja, from the island of Sulawesi (The Celebes).

***** ***** *****

In Europe, MTF priestesses served Artemis, Hecate and Diana. Early traditions thrived longest in Greece, and the mythology of the day encorporated (sic) tales of cross-dressing by Achilles, Heracles, Athena and Dionysus, as well as literal and metaphorical gender changes. * * * And Cupid was a dual god/dess of love, originally portrayed as intersex. The child of Hermes and Aphrodite, one of Cupid's variant names provided the origin for the term, "hermaphrodite."[215]

Another writer, Joshua J. Mark, also wrote about the religious history of bisexual and transgender practices. Mark, too, notes the Middle Eastern bisexual and transgender religious practices, writing that:

In ancient Mesopotamia, the priests and priestesses of the popular goddess Inanna (better known as Ishtar) were bisexual and transgender. According to their beliefs, the goddess had the power to transform

---

[215] Allen, Mercedes, "Trans History 101: Transgender Expression in Ancient Times", February 24, 2016 available at https://www.lgbtqnation.com/2016/02/trans-history-101-transgender-expression-in-ancient-times/

humans and could turn a man into a woman and a woman into a man. According to legend, the goddess's father created people of the third gender who were Inanna's servants. Non-binary identity existed over 3,000 years ago and was considered to be a manifestation of the divine will. The gods also blessed same-sex relationships as is clearly seen in the document The Almanac of Incantations, which contains prayers for both opposite and same-sex couples.[216]

Although not all Judeo-Christian faiths oppose, and many support, the two-gender position there is no doubt that both the two-gender and the transgender beliefs are in theological conflict with other religious orders. As competing theological views that have mixed theological reception and acceptance, neither the two-gender nor transgender religious beliefs should be taught in the public schools, proselytized using public funds, or depicted as "truth" by Federal, State or local governments. Again, it must be emphasized that society must not restrict or punish the practitioners of acts consistent with the Veejack religious beliefs or practices related to bisexual or transexual/transgender theory.

The Veejack religion also propagates views that conflict with Judeo-Christian theology through the use of taxes and government funding. The Veejack religion encourages a cycle of despair within those who view themselves as dependent on government assistance for survival. The Veejack faith also fosters within these communities a feeling of "victimhood" that justifies negative and immoral – even criminal – behavior. The VeeJack religion's goal is to create as many dependent voters as possible to ensure the election of the Veejack faith's believers. And, when the legal electorate experiences job growth, low inflation, and monetary accumulation of wealth the

---

[216] Mark, Joshua J., LGBTQ+ in the Ancient World, June 25, 2021 available at https://www.worldhistory.org/article/1790/lgbtq-in-the-ancient-world/

Veejack religion imports foreign undocumented paupers to generate the need for more taxes and organizations to spend taxpayer dollars. These organizations provide jobs for political workers who subscribe to the Veejack faith, who mask their Veejack religious proselytizing activities while pretending to assist the needy.

Many factions and sects within the Veejack religion are becoming openly antisemitic.[217] Commercial, cable, and social media in the Spring of 2024 are covering and broadcasting anti-Jewish / anti-Israel "demonstrations" that are too numerous to mention. On colleges and universities, the demonstrators are incorporating in their rhetoric and signage intense antisemitic slogans, threats, and violent behaviors. NPR, after interviews on college campuses, reported that there is:

> a spectrum of activity that could be considered antisemitic. And in general, those have fallen into three categories. First, there's been speech - targeted hate speech, protest slogans that may make some Jewish students feel unsafe, even speech that endorses the violence of Hamas. [218]

The Veejack religion's hatred of Jews also includes hatred of Christians and Christian institutions. While openly proselytizing the Veejack religion's texts and tenants in the public schools, the Veejack

---

[217] The Veejack religion is so opposed to Judaism that it accepts Hamas, Hezbollah, Isis and other vehemently anti-gay organizations as bedfellows under the theory that "the enemy of my enemy is my friend" even though these anti-Jewish organizations would brutally kill, without trial or mercy, all the Veejack religions' adherents who are gay, lesbian, bisexual, or transgender.

[218] Yousef, Odette and Hagen, Lisa, "Unpacking the truth of antisemitism on college campuses" April 25, 2024, NPR, at https://www.npr.org/2024/04/25/1247253244/unpacking-the-truth-of-antisemitism-on-college-campuses. However, media outlets that support Veejackian themes often fail to mention the antisemitism of the demonstrations. See, e.g., Lim, Clarissa-Jan, "NYPD Storms Columbia University, clears protesters from occupied building," May 1, 2024, MSNBC at https://www.msnbc.com/top-stories/latest/nypd-columbia-ccny-pro-palestinian-protests-arrests-rcna150185

faith's supporting elements constantly oppose public funding for Judeo-Christian schools.[219] The Veejack religion's policies also restrict the ability of Judeo-Christian institutions to raise money to help the poor and oppressed. By constantly advocating for increased taxation on workers, and by adopting economically inflationary monetary policies, the Veejack religion's elites reduce the discretionary income available to middle- and working-class Jews and Christians.[220] Where previously, Jews and Christians were actively donating to church-sponsored and other charitable organizations they no longer have the discretionary income to do so.

The Veejack religion, while hypocritically denying government funding to church-sponsored charities, funnels taxpayer dollars to innumerable charities that support the Veejack faith's values, projects, and goals. Where previously Jewish and Christian charities encouraged aid recipients to develop ethical behavior, adopt moral conduct, practice frugality, seek education, and obtain job skills, the Veejack faith's charities encourage recipients to view themselves as oppressed and dependent on the government.

One of the first theologians to identify the growth of the nascent faith was Sandra Schneiders.[221] Schneiders recognized that the United States mixes theology and law. Particularly, and unlike most other nations, the United States prohibits the government, and

---

[219] See, e.g., Fitzpatric, Cara, "The Charter-School Movement's New Divide – A Catholic charter in Oklahoma would represent a profound shift for American education—and for the charter-school movement itself," September 13, 2023, The Atlantic, at https://www.theatlantic.com/ideas/archive/2023/09/charter-schools-religion-public-secular/675293/

[220] Veejack's fondness for inflationary monetary policy is motivated, in part, by the "progressive" tax code that levies taxes on increased wages at a higher rate. Thus, by artificially increasing wages through inflation without a corresponding increase in buying power, Veejack imposes higher taxes on workers without having to achieve legislative enactments. Thus, the executive branch of government can increase the tax burden without involving the Congress. The individual Members of Congress welcome this "shell game" because they cannot then be criticized by their opponents for the harsh economic reality.

[221] See, e.g., Schneiders, 163-185.

its organizations, from establishing a religion. Since the goal of the Veejack religion is to inject itself into all levels of the government, and to control its funding, the Veejack religion's leadership early on recognized that it had to disguise itself; and that it must not adopt the public attributes of conventional religions. Through its stealth strategy the Veejack religion has inserted its ideology and beliefs into the mainstream of the culture of the United States. Especially, it has achieved widespread dissemination of its view through focusing on inserting its members in teaching positions in public schools, leadership positions in organizations providing social services, and civil service positions in governmental offices. The Veejack religion has used these positions of power to convert young people, provide aid to organizations that support the Veejack religion, and proselytize the public. The Veejack religion also uses the people it has inserted into these positions of educational leadership[222] and governmental power to criticize other religions, especially Judaism and Christianity. The impact of the Veejack religion's criticism of Christianity, for example, has contributed greatly to the phenomenon of the "nones" who have disaffiliated from Christianity.[223]

The key tenets of the Veejack religion are that it is non-theistic, elevates and describes its interpretations of science and reason as absolute "truth", denies religious mysticism while promoting an amorphous and undefined "spirituality", and has elastically fluid and evolving messaging. The Veejack religion's messaging changes and morphs as its leaders maneuver to achieve political and social power, manipulate governmental funding, achieve obedience from

---

[222] Veejack has consistently sought, under the guise of enhancing teacher's pay and benefits, to drain resources that would contribute to students' learning. This follows the practice Hoffer, at 137, noted early on, of movements exhibiting a "a diabolical realism . . . (that makes) all learning the monopoly of the elite which . . . (are) to rule . . . (and to) keep the anonymous masses barely literate."

[223] See, e.g., Stamps, Robert, *The Phenomenon of the Nones - And Faith in the Holy Spirit*, unpublished (a thesis paper presented to the Faculty of the Department of Theology, Loyola Marymount University In partial fulfillment of the Requirements for the degree Master of Arts in Theology).

its adherents, and further the weakening and even destruction of its religious competitors in the Jewish and Christian faiths.

The non-traditional "worship" spaces of the Veejack faith are social websites, the internet, broadcast media, email and other electronic messaging, musical concerts, and mass gatherings such as demonstrations, marches, and protests in streets, parks, and governmental and municipal buildings. More threatening to the social fabric of the United States is that the Veejack religion uses the public schools to proselytize and propagate its religious views under the guise that they are undisputed "truths". Through these organs and mechanisms, the Veejack religion exerts an outsized appeal and venue as it seeks its converts. The Veejack faith, echoing previous nontheistic religious outreach methods, concentrates especially on the lonely individual who feels outcast, neglected, or forlorn. The Veejack religion urges that it can provide a haven for those who feel their existence is meaningless and without form. With its use of the public schools as a pulpit the Veejack religion is rapidly converting generations of Americans to its views and values and generating increasing political strength.

Religions have values and beliefs that are central to their faith. Belief as a Christian is that Jesus Christ, who was crucified, died, and was buried, was resurrected, and achieved eternal life. This view is shared by all Christian faiths.[224] The Roman Catholic religious belief is that gender is immutable.[225] The Veejack religious belief, like that of the followers of the Mesopotamian goddess Ishtar, is that gender is fluid, and that human beings born male may transition to female, and human beings born female may transition to male.[226] The Roman Catholic religious view is that abortion is contrary to

---

[224] Matthew, Chapter 28; Mark, Chapter 16; Luke Chapter 24; John, Chapter 21; and Acts, Chapter 9.

[225] Declaration *Dignitas Infinita* On Human Dignity, Dicastery for the Doctrine of the Faith, April 8, 2024.

[226] https://en.wikipedia.org/wiki/Gender_fluidity

moral law.[227] Other Judeo-Christian faiths, while generally opposed to abortion, have a religious belief that abortion is appropriate sometimes.[228] The Veejack religious belief is that an abortion may be obtained at any time during gestation or at birth.[229] These various religious beliefs must be treated neutrally by the Federal and state governments. The Judeo-Christian faiths teach their adherents to honor their father and mother.[230] Contrary to this familial love, the Veejack religion's adherents are challenging whether a child's parents must be informed that their child is struggling with their

---

[227] Catechism of the Catholic Church, at 2270, 2271, 2272, and 2274; available at https://www.vatican.va/archive/ENG0015/_INDEX.HTM

[228] See, e.g., the discussion of the United Methodist Church's *Social Principles* at https://www.umc.org/en/content/ask-the-umc-what-is-the-united-methodist-position-on-abortion. It states that the United Methodist Church affirms the sanctity of life, and its "belief in the sanctity of unborn human life makes us reluctant to approve abortion," however, it believes they "are equally bound to respect the sacredness of the life and well-being of the mother . . .." See, also, Social Principles: The Nurturing Community - The Book of Discipline of The United Methodist Church – 2016, at https://www.umc.org/en/content/social-principles-the-nurturing-community#abortion, which states, "we recognize tragic conflicts of life with life that may justify abortion, and in such cases we support the legal option of abortion under proper medical procedures by certified medical providers."

[229] See, e.g., Associated Press, "Minnesota governor signs broad abortion rights bill into law", January 31, 2023, and Mekelburg, Madlin, "Do Democrats support abortion up until (and after) birth?", February 27, 2020, PolitiFact at https://www.politifact.com/factchecks/2020/feb/27/ted-cruz/do-democrats-support-abortion-until-and-after-birt/. This view is like the infanticide practiced in the ancient world, and most like the ancient Spartans in the Peloponnese. As recounted by History.com "(a)ll Spartan infants were brought before a council of inspectors and examined for physical defects, and those who weren't up to standards were left to die, and "(i)f a Spartan baby was judged to be unfit for its future duty as a soldier, it was most likely abandoned on a nearby hillside. Left alone, the child would either die of exposure or be rescued and adopted by strangers." See, e.g., Andrews, Evan, "8 Reasons It Wasn't Easy Being Spartan - From fitness tests for infants to state-sponsored hazing, find out why these ancient Greek warriors had a rough go of it", at https://www.history.com/news/8-reasons-it-wasnt-easy-being-spartan

[230] Exodus 20:12. This passage reads: "Honor your father and your mother, so that your days may be long in the land that the Lord your God is giving you."

gender identity.[231] While many adolescents struggle with questions of identity and gender it must be recognized that the Judeo-Christian religious belief and the Veejack religious belief offer two radically different responses and directions on how to proceed.[232] Thus, with at least two competing religious beliefs in opposition to each other, the public educational systems should not be teaching one or the other of the religious positions; nor should public educational institutions be involved.

Under the First Amendment to the United States Constitution the Federal and state governments may not favor one religion's belief over another religious belief.[233] The Judeo-Christian beliefs on the resurrection of Jesus to eternal life, gender immutability and opposition to abortion are not taught in the public schools because the First Amendment states the government shall make no law respecting an establishment of religion, nor should religion be taught in the public schools, or funded by the Federal or state governments. This same prohibition must be applied to the Veejack religion's beliefs on gender fluidity and easy access to abortion, which must be prohibited from being taught in the public schools or funded by the Federal or state governments. The Veejack religion, despite its political and economic power, must no longer be allowed to abuse the First Amendment prohibition on government making a law "respecting an establishment of religion."[234] The First Amendment prohibition on establishing a government religion is violated when the Veejack religious faith's teachings on gender, abortion and other issues are included in the curriculum in public schools, within

---

[231] See, e.g., Sawchuck, Stephen, "Are Teachers Obliged to Tell Parents Their Child Might Be Trans? Courts May Soon Decide," April 28, 2022, available at https://www.edweek.org/policy-politics/are-teachers-obliged-to-tell-parents-their-child-might-be-trans-courts-may-soon-decide/2022/04; and a version of this article appeared in the *June 01, 2022* edition of *Education Week* as *Are Teachers Obliged to Tell Parents Their Child Might Be Trans? Courts May Soon Decide.*

[232] Other religions, such as Islam, may have views like the Judeo-Christian view.

[233] See, the chapter on the First Amendment.

[234] U S Const. Amend. 1

legislative enactments, or through government grants to Veejack religious organizations.

The founding prophets of the movement that evolved into the United States' Veejack religion are Europeans Karl Marx and Friedrich Engels, and American Michael Harrington.[235] These early Veejack religious leaders criticized the Christian church and its leadership. Propaganda against Christianity helped expedite the exodus of the Nones from the Christian faith.[236] Their opposition to the concept of nation states resulted in their adherents who achieved political office implementing policies of "open borders" that led to unrestricted international migration and mass illegal immigration into the United States.[237]

The Veejack religion skillfully frightens its followers with apocalyptic visions involving the weather and climate. It utilizes normal variations in weather patterns and portrays them as alarming foretelling of societal doom and epochal destruction of the planet. The Veejack religion also imposes bizarre dietary and living habits on its adherents. The Veejack religion extracts money from its

---

[235] The nascent religious nature of the teachings of Marx and Engels was recognized as early as the late 18th century by scholars such as Ernest Renan, who recognized their teachings as leading to a religion of politics and economics. See, e.g., Hoffer, at 158.

[236] Propaganda against the Christian faith continues to this day. For example, when anti-Christian activists successfully argued that a Cross must be removed from public property after standing for fifty years one of the opponents' false arguments was that "the cross . . . had affiliation with the KKK." See, "Bay Area Christians fighting city which took down cross: 'They really hate what it stands for' – The cross on Albany Hill had stood for 52 years overlooking the East shore of San Francisco Bay," August 2, 2023 at https://www.foxnews.com/media/bay-area-christians-fighting-city-took-down-cross-really-hate-what-stands-for

[237] There is no Judeo-Christian principle on "open borders". One Catholic Priest explained there are three principles: People have the right to migrate to sustain their lives and the lives of their families; countries have the right to regulate their borders and to control immigration; and every country must regulate its borders with justice and mercy. See, Hewitt, Hugh, "Morning Glory: the border and 'Catholic social teaching' – If leftists tell you "Catholic social teaching" means an open border, they are either ignorant or lying," March 12, 2024 at https://www.foxnews.com/opinion/morning-glory-border-catholic-social-teaching

adherents, and shames the public if it, too, does not contribute to the apocalyptic "flavor of the month". The Veejack religion's ever-changing practice of shunning has previously forbidden its adherents and the public to wear animal fur, to purchase beef, ordered the elimination of plastic and certain fibers, championed fad diets, criticized petroleum products and gas-powered vehicles, demands taxpayers fund expensive and energy-deficient wind and solar farms, and sinks public funds into other useless endeavors owned and operated by Veejack faith leaders.

The Veejack religion mimics the Judeo-Christian concepts of mysticism, confession and prayer. For example, the song "When You Wish Upon a Star", from the 1940 Disney animated film "Pinocchio" is a classic of the genre of Veejack religious mysticism. This song asks its listeners to believe in magic. There are more Veejack religious hymns in the "wish" category that echo primitive religions and urge listeners to seek guidance from the stars, the moon, or the sun. Some Veejack religious songs even envision mystical genies who can provide gifts of money or items of value. Sadly, these pseudo-theistic fantasies rarely provide long-term solace to its adherents. As the Veejack faith refuses to admit its existence, and challenges Jewish and Christian practice's ability to soothe the human soul, its adherents are too often lonely, violent, and in need of institutionalization for mental trauma, and prone to suicide.

The Veejack religion's unique aspect of confession is to encourage its adherents to visit psychiatrists, psychics, psychologists, and to seek emotional solace by using mind-enhancing or soporific medicines and drugs.

The Veejack religion also has a pantheon of folk heroes. Many of its heroes are musical performers. The Veejack faith's leaders encourage its suburban and rural adherents to gather in primitive surroundings to sing folk songs to achieve communal bliss. A favorite of this branch of the Veejack religion is the song "I Dreamed I saw Joe Hill Last Night". The song is based on a poem by Alfred Hayes that honors labor activist Joe Hill who was executed for murder in

1915. It was turned into a song by Earl Robinson in 1936. Now the song is widely performed by the Veejack faith's musicians, and when sung by the Veejack faith's congregations in demonstrations, protests, and sit-ins induces a highly sought-after euphoria in the Veejack faith's adherents.[238]

For its urban adherents who do not share the rural fondness for folk music, the Veejack religion encourages chanting during demonstrations, much like the Braminic practice of emitting sacred sounds discussed earlier. The urban Veejack faithful enjoy chanting while linking arms in "chains" of demonstrators, or while shackling themselves to stationary public fixtures, defacing art and statues, or engaging in frantic activity such as during drug or alcohol-fueled musical concerts.

The Veejack faith's adherents participating in these activities seek a temporary euphoria as a replacement for the general emptiness of their lives. Both the rural and urban adherents of the Veejack religion also falsely believe that many common criminals who perform robbery, burglary, and other violent crimes are somehow "Robin Hood" figures who "rob from the rich to give to the poor", even though their victims are innocent and often severely injured or killed.[239]

---

[238] A version of the ballad "Joe Hill" was performed by Joan Baez at the famous Woodstock Festival in 1969. Available at https://www.youtube.com/watch?v=l-JW4DKxwQM. Ms. Baez' rendition contains the classic Veejack faith's resurrection equivalent in the first and closing verses:
> I dreamed I saw Joe Hill last night,
> alive as you and me.
> Says I "But Joe, you're ten years dead"
> "I never died" said he,
> "I never died" said he.

[239] See, e.g., folklorist Woody Guthrie's protest song romanticizing criminal killer, bank robber and outlaw Charles Arthur "Pretty Boy" Floyd in a song by describing Floyd's criminal behavior as generosity to the poor. A version by the folk-rock band "The Byrds" is available at https://www.bing.com/videos/search?q=byrids%20pretty%20boy%20flloyd%20videos&FORM=VIRE0&mid=B672B75F5FCC6C967997B672B75F5FCC6C967997&view=detail&ru=%2Fsearch%3Fq%3Dbyrids%20pretty%20boy%20flloyd.

Like the practice of "shunning" within many Judeo-Christian theologies, the followers of the Veejack faith encourage "cancelling" people who publicly criticize or differ from orthodox Veejackian religious beliefs.[240] The practice of shunning involved singling out a person, or group of people, for social rejection. In many cases, Judeo-Christian shunning required a formal ecclesiastical decision to cease interaction with an individual or group.[241] One of the most well-known examples of shunning occurs in Nathaniel Hawthorne's fictional 1850 novel *The Scarlet Letter*.[242] This novel recalls the shunning of a woman for perceived immoral conduct.

The Veejack religion's equivalent of shunning has been described as a "cancel culture."[243] The phenomenon of rejection and ostracism by the Veejack faith is inflicted on a person or group of people who act or speak in a manner that is unacceptable to orthodox religious Veejackianism. The cancellation is often publicly circulated through social media. Cancellation is most effective when used against elites and people who rely on the public for their livelihood; such as actors, comedians, musicians, and academics.

The Veejack religion uses the legal system as a form of coercion and to raise money. Wealthy Veejack religious elites finance legal suits alleging defamation to economically destroy their opponents,

---

[240] For a concise discussion of shunning, see, e.g., Sword, Rosemary K.M., and Zimbardo, Phillip, "Shunning: The Ultimate Rejection – What does it mean when we shun others or are shunned?", February 1, 2013, *Psychology Today*, at https://www.psychologytoday.com/us/blog/the-time-cure/201302/shunning-the-ultimate-rejection. See, also, Chapman, Fern Schumer, "How Religious Shunning Ruins Lives – A form of institutionalized estrangement, shunning hurts health of the excluded", March 27, 2024, *Psychology Today*, at https://www.psychologytoday.com/us/blog/brothers-sisters-strangers/202403/how-religious-shunning-ruins-lives.

[241] See, also, Blom, Phillip, *Nature's Mutiny – How the Little Ice Age of the Long Seventeenth Century Transformed the West and Shaped the Present*, New York: Liveright Publishing Corporation, 2019, at 206, for a description of the comprehensive ban placed on seventeenth century philosopher Baruch de Spinosa by a religious court in Amsterdam.

[242] Hawthorne, Nathaniel, "The Scarlet Letter," 2024 London: Penguin Classics.

[243] See, e.g., Cancel Culture at https://en.wikipedia.org/wiki/Cancel_culture

and Veejack religious district attorneys use outlandish legal theories to indict and send their opponents to trial. These tactics are reminiscent of the medieval witch trials that alleged possession of the person by the devil or the person engaging in some other unsanctioned, adulterous, or unapproved behavior.

The most pernicious of the Veejack faith's legal tactics is to file "class action" lawsuits that allege that governmental activity has harmed, or is harming, a large class of people. These lawsuits are usually frivolous and would be easily defended if the government attorneys chose to do so. However, the class action lawsuits are filed in districts that have elected officials that are sympathetic to the Veejack religion. The elected officials direct the government attorneys to "settle" the litigation for millions of dollars. Although the amount for individual plaintiffs is minimal, the percentage paid to the Veejack faith's lawyers filing the litigation is often substantial. The lawyers use the "settlement" money to finance Veejack religious activities. The taxpayers' money should not be used in this manner to fund Veejack religious activities.[244]

As author Fern Schumer Chapman observes, exclusion of a member of a faith is a social death penalty that results in long-term detrimental effects on mental health.[245] It is, Chapman notes, "a form of institutionalized estrangement and emotional abuse."[246]

For people who rely on the public for their livelihood cancellation by Veejack religious elites is often also an economic death penalty rendering the victim unable to earn a livelihood. Even in academia, where faculty in higher education are often granted tenure, the use of unapproved language to describe terms mandated by the Veejack religious elites, referring to gender, ethnicity, political beliefs, and other topics can result in termination. Once the unfortunate victim

---

[244] Please note that to be more specific about this societally harmful technique would invite litigation from the Veejack elected officials and attorneys that need to be exposed.

[245] Chapman, *Psychology Today*.

[246] Chapman, *Psychology Today*.

is terminated by Veejack religious elites the person is often unable to obtain other employment in academia. The inability of the cancelled academic to find another faculty position is due to the Veejack religion's almost universal control of academic institutions.[247]

The obverse of cancelation is the propensity of the Veejack religion's academic elites to champion the publications and speeches of other Veejack religious elites. This circular reinforcement gives the impression that Veejack religious beliefs are more popular and accepted than if the circular reinforcement did not exist. And the Veejack religion's professors and instructors often reward with higher grades those students who subscribe to the Veejack faith and participate in its sanctioned activities.[248]

---

[247] Notable exceptions to Veejack's widespread control of higher educational facilities in the United States are Judeo-Christian colleges and universities. The institutions of higher learning with Judeo-Christian roots are much more tolerant of diverse views, and openly encourage vigorous, polite debate within their constituencies. Some ostensibly Judeo-Christian institutions of higher learning, however, have unfortunately facilitated the stealth insertion of Veejackianism into their courses.

[248] Many of the sanctioned activities include protected demonstrations, and voter registration but often include illegal and/or violent activities as was observed in the antisemitic riots on college and university campuses in Spring 2024.

CHAPTER FIVE

GENERATING MASS MOVEMENTS AND DISCORD

The Veejack religion and its allies adopted a unique strategy to create an authoritarian movement and fulfill its goal of dismantling American social stability. During the late 1960s and early 1970s the writings of American social theorist and longshoreman Eric Hoffer became prominent in academia and warned against the nascent Veejack religion. Hoffer cautioned, in his book *The True Believer*, about the evils of fascism and how ordinary people had been persuaded to join in and tolerate its horrors.[249] Instead, however, of applying Hoffer's insights as a lens to recognize, and a methodology to thwart, future fascist mass movements, the VeeJack faith turned Hoffer's warnings about authoritarian movements on their head. In the Veejack faith's upside-down reality Hoffer's warnings became a blueprint for imposing the Veejack religion's agenda on American society. The Veejack religion also looked to linguistic theory to sow discord within American society.

Linguistically, English is a descendant of the Proto-Indo-European (PIE) languages that include many modern European and

---

[249] See, generally, Hoffer.

Indian subcontinent languages.[250] These languages evolved from the PIE language that flourished 5,000 years ago "in the steppes north of the Black and Caspian Seas in what is today southern Ukraine and Russia."[251] The PIE language "generate(d) daughter tongues that became the dominant languages spoken from Scotland to India."[252] The daughter tongues of the PIE language have several important characteristics that distinguish them from non-PIE tongues. Two of these characteristics that are common to all PIE daughter tongues are tense and number.

The Veejack religion and its supporters are forcefully and recklessly challenging linguistic tense and number. The ramifications of the Veejack religion's linguistic attack may have far reaching and unknown consequences. As American anthropologist David W. Anthony, an expert on Indo-European migrations and a student of linguistics, points out:

> . . . all Indo-European languages force the speaker to pay attention to tense and number when talking about an action: you *must* specify whether the action is past, present, or future; and you *must* specify whether the actor is singular or plural. It is impossible to use an Indo-European verb without deciding on these categories. Consequently speakers of Indo-European languages habitually frame all

---

[250] Language is so important that Durant, at 72, wrote that "(t)he beginning of humanity came when . . . (a person) squatted in a cave or in a tree, cracking . . . (his/her) brain to invent the first common noun, the first sound-sign that signify a group of objects . . .. * * * From that moment the mental development of . . . (humankind) opened upon a new and endless road. For words are to thought what tools are to work . . .."

[251] Anthony, David W., *The Horse the Wheel and Language – How Bronze-Age Riders from the Eurasian Steppes shaped the Modern World*, Princeton and Oxford: Princeton University Press, 2007, 5.

[252] Anthony, 8.

events in terms of when they occurred and whether they involved multiple actors.[253] (Italics in original)

The requirement to specify tense and number is not required in some non-PIE languages. For example, "when describing an event or condition in Hopi you *must* use grammatical markers that specify whether you witnessed the event yourself, heard about it from someone else, or consider it to be an unchanging truth."[254] Anthony speculates that "the constant and automatic use of such categories generates habits in the perception and framing of the world that probably differ between people who use fundamentally different grammars."[255]

One of the Veejack religion's key tenets is to abandon the English requirement to specify whether the actor is singular or plural. The Veejack faith demands and is imposing on public educational institutions and governmental offices that singular actors be addressed with the plural "they" rather than the traditional "he" or "she". Some Veejack religious adherents even use the plural "they" when speaking of themselves; as in substituting "they are" for "I am" as in "they are going to the store", when correct English grammar would specify the sentence as "I am going to the store." Notwithstanding the Veejack religion's attempt to disregard PIE convention, it is doubtful whether the Veejack religion's faithful would support Judeo-Christian individuals demanding they be addressed in the Biblical forms thee, thou, thy and thine for singular; and ye for plural.

In the Judeo-Christian tradition it has long been recognized that diverse languages can divide people. One of the oldest stories in the

---

[253] Anthony, 19.

[254] Anthony, 19. Please note that the Semitic language family is distinct from the Indo-European family. Semitic languages include Arabic, Hebrew, Amharic, and others. Arabic has a rich history and is widely spoken across the Middle East and North Africa. It has its own unique linguistic features, including a complex system of morphology and a distinctive script.

[255] Anthony, 19-20.

Bible describes the Tower of Babel and how a common language facilitated its growth. However, without a common language the peoples' project failed. The Bible describes it as:

> Now the whole earth had one language and the same words. And as they migrated from the east, they came upon a plain in the land of Shinar and settled there. And they said to one another, "Come, let us make bricks, and burn them thoroughly." And they had brick for stone, and bitumen for mortar. Then they said, "Come, let us build ourselves a city, and a tower with its top in the heavens, and let us make a name for ourselves; otherwise we shall be scattered abroad upon the face of the whole earth." The Lord came down to see the city and the tower, which mortals had built. And the Lord said, "Look, they are one people, and they have all one language; and this is only the beginning of what they will do; nothing that they propose to do will now be impossible for them. Come, let us go down, and confuse their language there, so that they will not understand one another's speech." So the Lord scattered them abroad from there over the face of all the earth, and they left off building the city. Therefore it was called Babel, because there the Lord confused the language of all the earth; and from there the Lord scattered them abroad over the face of all the earth.[256]

The attack on pronoun distinctions may seem trivial, but it is not.[257] In the aggregate the Veejack religion's attacks on the English

---

[256] Genesis 11:1-9.

[257] As Anthony, at 42, observes, "it took less than a thousand years for late Vulgate Latin to evolve into seven Romance languages . . .."

language and other areas of American culture are dangerous for American society.[258] As George Orwell, in his satirical futuristic novel *1984* [259] observed, the fictional fascists first want to destroy the language.[260] For example, in his novel Orwell has the repressive fictional dictatorial regime demand that the people eliminate words the regime considers dangerous; and the people must memorize falsehoods such as " War is peace – Freedom is Slavery – Ignorance is Strength."[261]

Removing words it considers hateful from the English language, changing grammar and confusing the distinction between singular

---

[258] In addition to changing the structure of language and definition of words, Veejack elites are also demanding the removal of statues that honor people of whom Veejack does not approve, and changing the names of geographic objects that honor conservative leaders. For example, the highest mountain in North America in Alaska was formerly named "Mount McKinley" to commemorate and honor William McKinley, who was President of the United States from 1897 until his brutal assassination in 1901 – and led the United States to economic prosperity and victory in the Spanish-American War. The mountain was renamed "Denali" under the pretext that Denali was its original name, although the tribal word "Denali" may actually have been a generic word meaning "mountain". By deleting the names of prominent conservatives from popular conversation, the Veejack elites hope to erase and/or rewrite history to their benefit. Parenthetically, as Durant observes at 60, in ancient times "many mountains were holy places, the homes of thundering gods." And, in the Bible at Exodus 3:1 Moses "came to Horeb, the mountain of God"; and at Exodus 19:20 "the Lord descended upon Mount Sinai." As with the Veejack religion, its colleagues in the Peoples Republic of China are trying to erase the minority Uyghur culture by changing ". . . the names of hundreds of villages in Xinjiang region in a move aimed at erasing Uyghur Muslim culture . . .." See, Lamche, Anna, "China changed village names 'to erase Uyghur culture'", June 20, 2024, BBC at https://www.bbc.com/news/articles/cxrrkl6ve39o

[259] Orwell, *1984*.

[260] See, e.g., Orwell, *1984*, at 7, where Orwell explains that the fictional dictatorial rulers forbade the speaking of words connected to freedom, democracy, and self-expression and adopted as the official language a dry, expressionless list of approved words known as "Newspeak". As Orwell explained in *1984*, at 284, "Newspeak was the official language . . . and had been designed to meet the ideological needs of . . . socialism." Orwell continued that "the purpose of Newspeak was . . . to provide . . . (an obedient) world view and mental habits . . . and to make all other modes of thought impossible."

[261] Orwell, *1984*, 8.

and personal pronouns are just a few examples of the Veejack religion's policies being inflicted on public educational institutions.[262] The preservation of the English language is absolutely essential for effective public education and preparing young people to find higher education, jobs, and advancement in society. Using grammatically correct English with regionally accepted pronunciation should be a key goal of public education. It is the key that unlocks the ability of speakers to communicate ideas, concepts, and actions. And the forcible abandonment of correct grammar in public education is enormously destructive to individuals and to society at large.[263]

A recent example of the Veejack faith adopting Orwellian tactics to change the English language was uncovered by podcaster Winston Marshall and revealed in a debate with former House of Representatives Speaker Nancy Pelosi hosted by the Oxford Union,

---

[262] Veejack has inculcated within its movement the goal of public educational institutions taking control over children and depriving parents of their right to teach their offspring. Veejack recognizes the accuracy of Hoffer's analysis, but instead of heeding it as a warning, Veejack uses Hoffer's cautionary words as a "how to" guide. Hoffer observed, at 36, that "mass movements show a hostile attitude towards the family by ". . . trying to discredit and disrupt it. They . . . (do it) by undermining the authority of the parents; by facilitating divorce; by taking over the responsibility for feeding, educating, and entertaining the children; and by encouraging illegitimacy." Orwell clairvoyantly predicted, in *1984*, at 284, religions like Veejack would destroy Judeo-Christian and Islamic family ties by imposing a belief to ". . . cut the links between child and parent, and between man and man, and between man and woman. (And impose a dystopian social order in which) no one dares trust a wife or child, or a friend any longer."

[263] Hoffer, at 137, explains that ". . . (would be dictators have) a diabolical realism . . . (and) plan to make all learning the monopoly of the elite which . . . (are) to rule . . . (and to) keep the anonymous masses barely literate." The Veejack religion, by capturing inner-city education, have kept the residents barely literate. One example of well-intentioned foolery is the Oakland, California School Board's attempt to recognize Ebonics, also known as African American English (AAE), as a language to be used in public schools. Rather than teaching students the standard English necessary to succeed in further education and employment, the Board wanted to maintain the legitimacy and richness of Ebonics as a language. See, e.g., https://en.wikipedia.org/wiki/African-American_Vernacular_English_and_social_context#Oakland_Ebonics_resolution; and https://en.wikipedia.org/wiki/Ebonics_(word).

at Oxford University in the United Kingdom.[264] In the debate, entitled "This House Believes Populism is a Threat to Democracy", Marshall argued that elites like Pelosi are trying to change the definition of the word "populism" for their political advantage.[265] Marshall demonstrated the elites tactics to change the accepted meaning of words, relating that:

> "'Populism' has become a word used synonymously with 'racist.' We've heard 'ethno-nationalist,' we have 'bigot,' we have 'hillbilly,' 'redneck,' we have 'deplorable,'" Marshall said. Pelosi had argued in her remarks that contemporary American populism currently had an ethno-nationalist character.

> "Elites use it to show their contempt for ordinary people," Marshall said.

> Marshall argued that the change in meaning of the word "populist" is "a recent change," and pointed to a 2016 speech delivered by then-President Barack Obama, who he said "took umbrage with the notion that Trump be called a populist."

> "If anything, Obama argued that he (Obama) was the populist. If anything, Obama argued that Bernie (Sanders) was the populist," he said. "Something curious happens. If you watch Obama's speeches after that point, more and more recently, he uses the word 'populist' interchangeably with 'strong

---

[264] Morris, Kyle, "Pelosi rebuked to her face during Oxford debate after condemning Americans clouded by 'guns, gays, God' – Pelosi suggested Americans refuse to listen to Democrats about certain issues due to their beliefs about 'guns, gays, [and] God'", May 11, 2024, Fox News at https://www.foxnews.com/politics/pelosi-rebuked-oxford-debate-condemning-americans-clouded-guns-gays-god
[265] *Id.*

man,' 'authoritarian.' The word changes meaning.
It becomes a negative, a pejorative, a slur."[266]

The implications for American political dialogue are frightening. Veejack religious elites must not be permitted to use public educational institutions to retroactively change the meanings of words or abolish tense and number. The cynical manipulation of vocabulary, forewarned by George Orwell in his novel *1984*, is covertly creeping into all aspects of American political dialogue to benefit Veejack religious goals. Marshall clearly encapsulated the danger, noting "that 'populism is the voice of the voiceless' and that the 'real threat to democracy is from the elites.'"[267]

In addition to changing the definition of common terms, the Veejack religion's elites are adopting the Orwellian technique of retroactively changing history and are attempting to confuse reality and fiction. As Orwell noted, ". . . the chosen lie would become truth."[268] One classic example is Democratic President Joseph "Joe" Biden's insistence in repeated interviews that the rate of inflation was 9% when he began his presidency. Even network CNN, which is generally helpful to Democratic politicians, had to admit the falsity of the President's claim. CNN wrote:

> For the second time in less than a week, President Joe Biden falsely claimed Tuesday that the inflation rate was 9% when he began his presidency.
>
> Biden was criticized by many Republicans, including former president and current presidential rival Donald Trump, for telling CNN in an interview last Wednesday: "No president's had the run we've had in terms of creating jobs and bringing

---

[266] *Id.*

[267] *Id.*

[268] Orwell, *1984*, 45.

down inflation. It was 9% percent when I came to office, 9%."

Biden repeated the claim about the inflation rate, albeit in slightly vaguer form, in a Tuesday interview with Yahoo Finance. This time, he said: "I think inflation has gone slightly up. It was at 9% when I came in, and it's now down around 3%."[269]

The claim by President Biden was so extreme that CNN felt compelled to add an additional qualifier that "Biden's claim that the inflation rate was 9% when he became president is not close to true. The year-over-year inflation rate in January 2021, the month of his inauguration, was about 1.4%."[270] CNN explained that President Biden's "claims make it sound like inflation is much lower today than it was when he was inaugurated – but it is actually higher . . .".[271] And this was not President Biden's first attempt to rewrite history. CNN noted that "Biden's false claims in the past week about overall inflation are similar to a false claim he made in October 2022 when talking about gas prices in particular. In both cases, he has wrongly depicted a figure from June 2022 as if it was the Biden-era starting point."[272] As Orwell in the novel *1984* describes the repressive fictional dictators who adjusted figures to suit their needs, they would substitute "one piece of nonsense for another."[273]

---

[269] Dale, Daniel, "Fact check: Biden again falsely claims inflation was 9% when he became president", May 14, 2024, CNN Facts First at https://www.cnn.com/2024/05/14/politics/fact-check-biden-inflation-when-he-became-president?cid=ios_app

[270] *Id.*

[271] *Id.*

[272] *Id.*

[273] Orwell, *1984*, 42. As the novel's protagonist, Winston Smith, at 148, explains to his girlfriend "(e)very record has been destroyed or falsified, every book has been rewritten, every picture has been repainted, every statue and street and building has been renamed, every date has been altered." Today, across the southern United

The Veejack religion strives to divide people on the basis of race, ethnicity, sex and sexual orientation, religion, wealth, geography, and other human characteristics. Quoting Ernest Renan, Hoffer explained – and the Veejack religion adopted as a guiding tenet - that "fanatics . . . fear liberty more than they fear persecution."[274] Helping the Veejack religion locate the potential fanatics, Hoffer unintentionally pointed out where to recruit new members. And that is where the Veejack religious recruiters concentrate on finding disaffected people for its movement. As noted earlier, Hoffer explained:

> the disaffected are found in all walks of life, they are most frequent in the following categories: (a) the poor, (b) misfits, (c) outcasts, (d) minorities, (e) adolescent youth, (f) the ambitious . . . (g) those in the grip of some vice or obsession, (h) the impotent . . . (i) the inordinately selfish, (j) the bored, (and) (k) the sinners.[275]

As with all new religions, the Veejack faith exemplifies Hoffer's recognition that "a rising religious movement is all change and experiment – open to new views and techniques from all quarters."[276] The Veejack faith also seeks to instill depression and futility in peoples' minds and remove aspiration and higher goals. The Veejack religion does this because, as Hoffer noted, "(w)here self-advancement

---

States historical statues are being removed, and books banned, to satisfy the demands of Veejack enthusiasts. See, e.g., Rhoden, Giselle and Paul, Dalila, "73 Confederate monuments were removed or renamed last year, report finds", February 3, 2022, CNN at https://www.cnn.com/2022/02/02/us/confederate-monuments-removed-2021-whose-heritage/index.html; and Powell, Alvin, September 28, 2000, "Fight over Huck Finn continues: Ed School professor wages battle for Twain classic", The Harvard Gazette at https://news.harvard.edu/gazette/story/2000/09/fight-over-huck-finn-continues-ed-school-professor-wages-battle-for-twain-classic/

[274] Hoffer, 32.

[275] Hoffer, 32.

[276] Hoffer, 4.

cannot, or is not allowed to, serve as a driving force, other sources of enthusiasm have to be found . . .."[277] The new enthusiasms are often "religious, revolutionary and nationalist movements . . .."[278]

After the Veejack religion has demolished its adherents' feelings of self-worth and individualism, it stimulates their frustration. The Veejack religion manipulates people using Hoffer's analysis as a guide by recognizing that:

> the frustrated, oppressed by their shortcomings, blame their failure on existing restraints. Actually, their innermost desire is for an end to the 'free for all.' They want to eliminate free competition and the ruthless testing to which the individual is continuously subjected in a free society.[279]

The Veejack faith believes that the United States is a flawed society. As a revolutionary religious movement, the Veejack religious movement seeks to generate a new anti-Constitutional, and self-destructive nationalism. For, as Hoffer explained, "nationalism is the most copious and durable source of mass enthusiasm" and "nationalist fervor must be tapped if the drastic changes projected and initiated by revolutionary enthusiasm are to be consummated."[280]

Orwell, prescient as ever, recognized that new authoritarian movements like the Veejack religion would employ rhythmical chants and tom-toms to generate emotion and impose "a self-hypnosis, a deliberate drowning of consciousness by means of rhythmic noise."[281] In *1984* Orwell anticipated the Veejack religion's beliefs that its elites are superior, writing that "(t)he Party taught that proles[282] were natural inferiors who must be kept in subjection, like animals" and

---

[277] Hoffer, 3.

[278] Hoffer, 3.

[279] Hoffer, 33.

[280] Hoffer, 4.

[281] Orwell, *1984*, 19

[282] In Orwell, *1984*, "proles" is the term for common or poor people.

"(s)o long as they continued to work and breed, their other activities were without importance."[283]

The Veejack religious elites have adopted the belief of the fictional autocrats in the novel *1984* that "(i)t was not desirable that the proles should have strong political feelings . . . (just) a primitive patriotism which could be appealed to . . .."[284] The proles were allowed to indulge in "criminality . . . (and were) thieves, bandits, prostitutes, drug-peddlers, and racketeers of every description; but since it all happened among the proles themselves, it was of no importance. In all questions of morals, they were allowed to (do as they pleased)" and the "sexual puritanism of the Party was not imposed on them."[285] Thus it is with the Veejack faith and its belief that people in the ghetto may engage in criminality without consequences; provided the victims are other ghetto-dwellers or members of the work force.

The Veejack religion subscribes to the principle that its elites must retain their elite status to the exclusion of the poor and the workers. This is because, as Orwell relates about wealth in the novel *1984*:

> If it once became general, wealth would confer no distinction. It was possible, no doubt, to imagine a society in which wealth, in the sense of personal possessions and luxuries, should be evenly distributed, while power remained in the hands of a small privileged caste. But in practice such a society could not long remain stable. For if leisure and security were enjoyed by all alike the great mass of human beings who are normally stupefied by poverty would become literate and would learn

---

[283] Orwell, *1984*, 70. Veejack, feeding off the working class, adopts Orwell's dystopian dictate, but substitutes welfare for work. Nevertheless, Veejack maintains ghettos to contain subservient people whose only role is to vote Veejack adherents into positions of authority.

[284] Orwell, *1984*, 71.

[285] Orwell, *1984*, 71.

to think for themselves; and when once they had done this, they would sooner or later realize that the privileged minority had no function, and they would sweep it away. In the long run, a hierarchical society was only possible on a basis of poverty and ignorance.[286]

The Veejack religion cynically and falsely preaches that its Judeo-Christian political opponents are dictatorial and criminal and must be eliminated. To forestall complacency the Veejack faith urges its adherents to reject personal advancement and to, instead, mold a new order.[287] As Hoffer observed, "those who see their lives as spoiled and wasted crave equality and fraternity more than they do freedom."[288] Thus the Veejack religion employs riotous demonstrations and the takeover of streets, parks, and other public places to instill a feeling of mutual association within its adherents. As Orwell recounted in *1984*, the leadership in his novel's dystopian society regularly conducted a spasm of hate. Stylized as "(t)he Two Minutes of Hate (it) brought about within the people . . . fear and

---

[286] Orwell, *1984*, 181. This dictum is covertly promoted by Veejack. Its promotion by Veejack explains why the poor in the United States, despite the enormous amount of money being spent on public education, remain largely illiterate. The primary benefit of money spent on public education goes not to educating the students, but to enriching those who control the buildings, grounds, faculty, and significantly, the administrators and their political lobbyists.

[287] Hoffer, at 13, points out that "When a mass movement begins to attract people who are interested in their individual careers, it is a sign that it has passed its vigorous stage; that it is no longer engaged in molding a new world but in possessing and preserving the present." Another guiding principle for Veejack's recruitment is Hoffer's observation, at 35, that:

The ideal potential convert is the individual who stands alone, who has no collective body he can blend with and lose himself in and so mask the pettiness, meaninglessness, and shabbiness of his individual existence. Where a mass movement finds the corporate pattern of family, tribe, country, etcetera, in a state of disruption and decay, it moves in and gathers the harvest. Where it finds the corporate pattern in good repair, it must attack and disrupt.

[288] Hoffer, 33.

vindictiveness, a desire to kill, to torture, to smash faces with a sledgehammer . . . (turning each one) into a grimacing, screaming lunatic."[289] The Veejack religion routinely uses the tactic of public hysteria, shouting, violence, and destruction to both motivate its adherents and instill fear in the community.

Another recruiting tool adopted by the Veejack religion is recognition that Hoffer was correct when he noted that "boredom accounts for the almost invariable presence of spinsters and middle-aged women at the birth of mass movements."[290] Orwell was more inclusive than Hoffer, writing that with fascism, "(i)t was always the women, and above all the young ones, who were the most bigoted adherents of the Party, the swallowers of slogans, the amateur spies and nosers-out of unorthodoxy."[291] And the Veejack religion's angry, and often violent, demonstrations often place women in vulnerable positions during demonstrations to curry sympathy from the public when they are inevitably injured and/or arrested.[292]

As an incentive and to establish role models, the Veejack religion relentlessly honors those who throw their lives away in riotous and/ or criminal behavior. The Veejack religion's faithful praises them, aping Hoffer's observation that authoritarian leaders often inspire their followers with slogans like "we cannot be sure that we have something worth living for unless we are ready to die for it."[293]

---

[289] Orwell, *1984*, 17.

[290] Hoffer, 52.

[291] Orwell, *1984*, 13.

[292] As part of its strategy for demonstrations Veejack elites very cleverly stage-managed the COVID epidemic to achieve two advantages. Threats of catching a communicable disease so unnerved the public that Veejack elites demanded they wear masks. Though medical experts differed on whether masks were effective to prevent COVID the primary benefit was not medical; it was political: overturning a centuries-old public policy against wearing masks in public. Because of the Veejack elites' scare tactics about COVID, people can now routinely go "masked" in public. Thus, in demonstrations and other rowdy pro-Veejack antics the perpetrators are masked so that the police and news media are unable to identify and punish them.

[293] Hoffer, 16. Sadly, Veejack's followers who heed the advice to suffer, and perhaps die, for Veejack are but easily sacrificed pawns in the eyes of the Veejack elites. The

The Veejack faith's leaders heed and seek to implement within the United States Hoffer's dictum that "(n)ot only does a mass movement depict the present as mean and miserable – it deliberately makes it so."[294] And, Hoffer further observed, the mass movement "fashions a pattern of individual existence that is dour, hard, repressive and dull."[295] The Veejack religion instills in its followers a complete absence of value for the present. Sadly, the Veejack religion teaches its followers, as Hoffer observed of many mass movements, to view "ordinary enjoyment as trivial or even discreditable, and . . . the pursuit of personal happiness as immoral."[296]

Rather than heed Hoffer's warning about fanaticism and its self-destructive tendencies, the Veejack religion wants its followers to "see their lives and the present as spoiled beyond remedy and . . . (be) ready to waste and wreck both: hence their recklessness and their will to chaos and anarchy."[297] The Veejack religion wants its followers to seek the "sheltering and soothing anonymity of a communal existence."[298] Again reversing the warning Hoffer expressed about mass movements, the Veejack faith has vigorously adopted Hoffer's admonition that "it is futile to judge the viability of a new movement by the truth of its doctrine and the feasibility of its promises. What has to be judged is its corporate organization for quick and total absorption of the frustrated."[299] And in this area the Veejack religion has steadily broadened its corporate organization while keeping it sequestered from the public and virtually unknown to the people that the Veejack faith is successfully manipulating.

---

sacrifice of a Veejack follower elicits from an elite hardly more than a "tut, tut" over a glass of wine or slice of cheesecake, if the person is remembered at all.

[294] Hoffer, 69.
[295] Hoffer, 69.
[296] Hoffer, 69.
[297] Hoffer, 24-25.
[298] Hoffer, 38.
[299] Hoffer, 41.

CHAPTER SIX

VEEJACK RELIGIOUS PRACTICES AND VALUES

The Veejack religion's followers include many factions and sects. Several reject the eating and/or use of animal products. The most restrictive Veejack religious sect, who have coopted and use the term "vegans" to refer to themselves, rejects the use of animal products for any purpose. A lesser restrictive Veejack faction, which has also coopted and uses the term "vegetarians" to refer to its adherents, rejects the eating of meat. However, many of the Veejack vegetarians will consume dairy products, such as milk, eggs, butter, and ice cream and accept the use of animal products in clothing, shoes, and handbags, etc. While some vegans and vegetarians have adopted their restrictive diet for health purposes, many vegans and vegetarians have adopted their beliefs as part of their adherence to a Veejack religious sect's teachings of "truth". The various Veejack religious sects' teachings on vegan and vegetarian lifestyles, which are aspects of the Veejack religious faith, must also be banned from public schools, prohibited in brochures or pamphlets presented to recipients of government assistance, or supported by public funding.

The Judeo-Christian religion teaches that God created the animal kingdom, including birds, fish and other creatures, for the benefit of humankind. The Bible reveals:

> Then God said, "Let us make humankind in our image, according to our likeness; and let them have dominion over the fish of the sea, and over the birds of the air, and over the cattle, and over all the wild animals of the earth, and over every creeping thing that creeps upon the earth."

> So God created humankind in his image,
> in the image of God he created them;
> male and female he created them.

> God blessed them, and God said to them, "Be fruitful and multiply, and fill the earth and subdue it; and have dominion over the fish of the sea and over the birds of the air and over every living thing that moves upon the earth." God said, "See, I have given you every plant yielding seed that is upon the face of all the earth, and every tree with seed in its fruit; you shall have them for food. And to every beast of the earth, and to every bird of the air, and to everything that creeps on the earth, everything that has the breath of life, I have given every green plant for food.[300]

In the Judeo-Christian Old Testament, God discusses religious offerings. God explains that animals shall be sacrificed and smoked. This is because when meat is burned on the alter, the "smoke . . . (from) the burnt offering that is on the wood of the fire . . . (is a)

---

[300] Genesis 1:26-30.

pleasing odor to the Lord."[301] The Judeo-Christian God, however, directed that only certain meats could be eaten.[302] Specifically, God commanded them not to eat any "abhorrent thing", and described the animals, fish, and birds that should be consumed.[303] For Christians, the New Testament picks up and eliminates most dietary restrictions on animal products. Saint Peter, in a vision, learns that the dietary laws set forth in Leviticus and Deuteronomy are no longer applicable and that all animal products from then on are available for use.[304] And the Apostles in a Council in Jerusalem led by Jesus' brother James recognized that non-Jewish converts to Christianity did not have to adopt Jewish dietary restrictions.[305]

As opposed to the Veejack religious sect's vegan and vegetarian sects, the Judeo-Christian practice authorizes the eating of meat and use of animal products. These are competing Veejack religious and Judeo-Christian religious beliefs and practices. For this reason, Veejack religious sect's vegan and vegetarian practices should not be taught in the public schools or proselytized by government through the use of government funds.

Most importantly, Jesus told the parable of the prodigal son who claimed his inheritance from his father and left his father's home.[306] The son became destitute and lower than the lowest workers on his father's land, so he returned home to beg his father to let him have a job. Instead, his father – who in Jesus' parable represents God – welcomed the young man home and ordered that the fatted calf be

---

[301] Leviticus 3:5.

[302] Leviticus 11

[303] Deuteronomy 14:3-21. Islam also has laws that Muslims follow in their diet. Islamic jurisprudence specifies which foods are halāl (lawful) and which are harām (unlawful). Muslims are allowed to eat what is "good" (Quran 2:168). Muslims do not consume pork or alcohol and mandate that a humane process be used for the slaughter of animals for meat. The dietary laws are found in the Quran, the holy book of Islam, as well as in collections of traditions attributed to Islamic prophet Muhammad ("Sunnah").

[304] Acts 10:9-16, 28.

[305] Acts 15.

[306] Luke 15:11-32.

killed and prepared for a sumptuous dinner. A fatted calf is veal; one of the tastiest foods from the animal kingdom.

Thus, when the subsects of the Veejack religion extoll their vegan or vegetarian practices and impliedly or directly criticize the Judeo-Christian beliefs on the animal kingdom as a benefit to be used by mankind, they are proselytizing their religious practices in a forum to which the Judeo-Christian teachings are excluded. The teachings of the Veejack religion must also be excluded from these government-sponsored activities.

CHAPTER SEVEN

CLIMATE AND THE WEATHER GODS

Planet Earth is experiencing a warming trend. There is no doubt that globally the Earth's climate is getting warmer. The warming trend, however, is not caused by mankind. The warming of planet Earth has been occurring for almost twelve thousand years since the end of the Ice Age;[307] and more recently the end of the seventeenth century Mini Ice Age.[308] The contribution of human activity to the warming trend is minimal, if occurring at all. Yet, for political and economic advancement, powerful members of the Veejack faith are blistering the public with farcical pronouncements that humankind must not only alter its behavior but must pay enormous sums of money to the Veejack faith's elites. Through its protected status as a stealth religion, the Veejack faith is furthering its false claims that human activity is the cause of global warming. The Veejack religion is skillfully manipulating the fallacious fable that humans cause global warming in order to obtain almost complete control

---

[307] The Last Glacial Period (LGP), also known colloquially as the Last Ice Age or simply Ice Age, occurred from the end of the Last Interglacial to the end of the Younger Dryas, encompassing the period c. 115,000 – c. 11,700 years ago. See, e.g., https://en.wikipedia.org/wiki/Last_Glacial_Period

[308] See, e.g., Blom.

of government within the United States. The Veejack religion uses this control to influence the texts used in public education,[309] and critical functions of governmental legislation, administration, and grant funding.

The ancient Greeks, who laid the foundation for Western culture, believed that there were four basic environmental elements: earth, air, fire, and water. Early Hindu and Buddhist teachings, as well as those of African and Native American peoples, shared this concept of four basic environmental elements.[310] Modern society, in its efforts to control its own environment, should remember and respect the wisdom of these early understandings of nature. Rather than trying to impact the weather or change the climate, modern

---

[309] Veejack's control of public education furthers its goal of maintaining an uneducated public. Veejack's control of public education is also a leading cause of anxiety and depression in young adults. By hijacking public education and preaching its depressing, nihilistic, nontheistic theology doctrines to young Americans Veejack is directly responsible for the youth mental health crises. See, e.g., "Mental Health Challenges of Young Adults Illuminated in New Report – Making Caring Common identifies several drivers of young adults' emotional challenges, including a lack of meaning and purpose," October 24, 2023, posted by News Editor, Harvard Graduate School of Education at https://www.gse.harvard.edu/ideas/news/23/10/mental-health-challenges-young-adults-illuminated-new-report. This report identifies that young adults' mental health challenges include:

A lack of meaning, purpose, and direction: Nearly 3 in 5 young adults (58%) reported that they lacked "meaning or purpose" in their lives in the previous month. Half of young adults reported that their mental health was negatively influenced by "not knowing what to do with my life."

Financial worries and achievement pressure: More than half of young adults reported that financial worries (56%) and achievement pressure (51%) were negatively impacting their mental health.

A perception that the world is unraveling: Forty-five percent (45%) of young adults reported that a general "sense that things are falling apart" was impairing their mental health.

Relationship deficits: Forty-four percent (44%) of young adults reported a sense of not mattering to others and 34% reported loneliness.

Social and political issues: Forty-two percent (42%) reported the negative influence on their mental health of gun violence in schools, 34% cited climate change, and 30% cited worries that our political leaders are incompetent or corrupt.

[310] Classical Elements at https://en.wikipedia.org/wiki/Classical_element

society must concentrate instead on trying to clean and maintain its own earth, air, fire, and water.

For the United States this means concentrating on removing garbage, grime, and hazardous substances from the cities, suburbs, farms, forests, plains, meadows, and waters. The air must be protected from contaminants as was done when the ozone layer was threatened, and the international community worked together to create the *Montreal Protocol*[311] that banned halogenated hydrocarbons that deplete stratospheric ozone.

The ancient element of fire creates contaminants that arise from volcanoes, forest fires, smokestacks, vehicle exhausts, residences, and from natural sources of emission.[312] Creative forest management, which adopts controlled burns and other preventive measures, reduces the occurrence of catastrophic fires. Exhaust from manmade sources such as petroleum, coal and natural gas can be controlled. Bodies of still and flowing water can be cleaned to maintain aquatic life by addressing specific problems.[313] However, political motives for personal profit such as banning coal in favor of expensive and immature industries like solar and wind power or eliminating petroleum powered vehicles in favor of expensive battery powered vehicles, just shifts the pollution without eliminating it.

The Veejack religion's opposition to the use of carbon produced

---

[311] *1987 Montreal Protocol on Substances that Deplete the Ozone Layer*, 1522 UNTS 3, 26 ILM 1541, 1550 (1987). The Conference of Plenipotentiaries on the Protocol on Chlorofluorocarbons to the Vienna Convention for the Protection of the Ozone Layer was held in Montreal, Canada from 14-16 September 1987.

[312] Methane in the atmosphere is accused of contributing to global warming. However, 40% of methane emissions into the atmosphere occur from natural sources. See, e.g., Gerretsen, Isabelle; Henriques, Martha; Bourke, India; and Sherriff, Lucy, "Exploding craters and overflowing landfills are unexpected sources of methane," April 3, 2024 at https://www.bbc.com/future/article/20240402-the-surprising-sources-of-methane

[313] When a sea turtle was discovered with a plastic straw in its nostril "the anti-plastic-straw movement caught the world's attention" and cleanup efforts began. See, Rosch, Carla, "The bloody turtle video that sparked a plastic straw revolution," April 9, 2024 at https://www.bbc.co.uk/future/article/20240402-the-turtle-video-that-sparked-a-plastic-straw-revolution

by coal-powered plants and gasoline-powered transportation vehicles does not help the environment.[314] The Veejack religion's opposition to carbon is designed to both increase the power of its elites to control the public and to intimidate the public into obedience and submission to Veejack's religious dictates. Banning coal in the United States does not significantly impact the world's atmosphere. The United States, previous to the Veejack religion's imposition of a hysterical anti-coal culture in the populace was the world's leader in "clean burning" coal. By eliminating coal and gasoline-powered transportation within the United States in favor of electrically powered transportation vehicles, the Veejack religion's elites have shifted industrial manufacture of transportation vehicles, and the batteries that power them, to China. China consumes almost ten times as much coal as the United States and burns the coal in plants that are not clean. Instead, China uses some of the dirtiest coal plants in the world.[315]

The International Energy Agency (IEA) issues reports on the consumption of coal worldwide and issued its most recent report for 2023.[316] As related by the IEA, China is a huge consumer of coal:

> Accounting for more than half of global coal demand, China is by far the world's largest coal consumer. In 2022, the country's overall coal demand rose by 4.6% to a total of 4 520 Mt, with coal taking a share of more than 60% in power generation. India, the world's second-largest coal consumer comprising about 14% of global coal demand, recorded an increase of 9%, totaling 1,162 Mt.[317]

The Veejack religious elites try to instill terror and obedience

---

[314] Veejack's policies in other environmental arenas are also counterproductive and potentially catastrophic; such as opposition to controlled burns in forests.

[315] International Energy Agency (December 2023) at https://www.iea.org/data-and-statistics/charts/global-coal-consumption-2020-2023

[316] https://www.iea.org/reports/coal-2023

[317] https://www.iea.org/reports/coal-2023/demand

in the populace of the United States with dire warnings about how the use of coal is contaminating the environment. The Veejack religion's elites castigate the people of the United States for accepting the benefits that coal provides such as warm housing during the winter; hot water for bathing; and electricity to power household and other appliances. The Veejack religious elites vigorously rail against the use of coal and gasoline-powered transportation vehicles within the United States, but their opposition does not help the world environment. Instead, their opposition to the use of coal and gasoline-powered transportation vehicles within the United States accelerates the use of coal and gasoline in China. And China is the worst coal polluter in the world.

Retaining the use of coal and gasoline powered transportation vehicles within the United States actually helps the environment. This is because the United States is committed to and has developed the cleanest coal burning plants in the world. The United States has also developed methods for transportation vehicles to use gasoline and diesel fuels in a clean manner. Pollution from vehicles powered by petroleum products can be eliminated by investing in environmentally safe engines and exhaust systems. In the future, electric vehicles may be produced at a price and convenience that competes with petroleum powered vehicles and that do not spontaneously explode; or may be manufactured without using dangerous metals or chemicals; and do not generate manufacturing-source pollution. If that time arrives, then consumers will purchase electric vehicles. Until that time comes it is dangerous to the environment to pretend that electric vehicles can provide efficient transportation without pollution.

Water falls to the earth in the form of rain, sleet, and snow and nestles in the air as humidity and fog. On the surface of the earth water resides in oceans, lakes, ponds, rivers, streams, and reservoirs. Water is precious for sustaining human life. Water provides an environment for fish and other sea creatures to thrive; as a transportation surface for boats, barges, and ship; and in the polar ice caps the earth's climatic history can be tracked. Water in flowing rivers generates electric power, in all its forms it provides a place for human recreation, and it is a source and location for myriad other uses.

It is important to note that the earth is indeed warming. However, earth's warming is not due to human activity. Earth is still cycling out of the most recent Ice Age and is recovering from the Mini Ice Age.[318]

The cause of the Mini Ice Age, like the unusually cool weather in the mid-fourth century CE that led to the decline of the Roman Empire, has not been determined.[319] Some theorists believe the Mini Ice Age was caused by the eruption of Peruvian volcano Mount Huaynaputina in 1600.[320] Others believe it may have been caused by sunspots – or rather the lack of sunspots.[321] While data is limited for the mid-Fourth century cooling, there is "abundant evidence" about the Mini Ice Age though "there is little understanding of exactly why it occurred."[322] Despite the Mount Huaynaputina theory for

---

[318] See, e.g., Blom.

[319] Blom, 12-13.

[320] Blom, 43. Another volcanic eruption that altered the weather for as many as 1,500 years was the eruption over 74,000 years ago known as the Toba Eruption. This eruption in modern day Sumatra, Indonesia, was "one of the largest known explosive eruptions in the Earth's history." The impact on earth's climate of the Toba Eruption is being debated, and much evidence exists of its impact on climate. The impact was immense. Wikipedia writes: "The outflow sheet originally covered an area of 20,000–30,000 km2 (7,700–11,600 sq mi) with thickness nearly 100 m (330 ft), likely reaching into the Indian Ocean and the Straits of Malacca. The air-fall of this eruption blanketed the Indian subcontinent in a layer of 5 cm (2.0 in) ash, the Arabian Sea in 1 mm (0.039 in), the South China Sea in 3.5 cm (1.4 in), and Central Indian Ocean Basin in 10 cm (3.9 in). Its horizon of ashfall covered an area of more than 38,000,000 km2 (15,000,000 sq mi) in 1 cm (0.39 in) or more thickness." See, "Youngest Toba Eruption," Wikipedia at https://en.wikipedia.org/wiki/Youngest_Toba_eruption

[321] Blom, at 229, explains that "the lack of sunspots is known as the Maunder Minimum" and "from 1645 to 1715 (the lack of sunspots) coincided with the greatest extended period of temperature reduction."

[322] Blom, 13. For instance, Blom at 147, notes that in mid-seventeenth century Sweeden the average temperature was on average two degrees Celsius colder than the

the cause of the Mini Ice Age, Europe did not experience its coldest winter until more than half a century later, in 1684.[323] We know there was a Mini Ice Age that cooled the earth, but science has not determine why it occurred.

During the Mini Ice Age, the unusually cold weather may have contributed to the arctic winds' destruction in 1588 of the Spanish Armada King Phillip II of Spain sent to conquer Queen Elizabeth's England.[324] The Mini Ice Age also caused the Thames River in London to freeze solid more than twelve times between 1565 and 1695, which was more than double the rate of freezing over the previous 150 years.[325] The year 1816 was known as the "year without a summer".[326] The Mini Ice Age caused bad harvests in Europe, which led, in that "religious and superstitious age", to a "collective hysteria (and) witch trials."[327]

The Veejack religion's response to the general warming trends occasioned by the end of the classical Ice Age of twelve thousand years ago and the still-present aftereffects of the tapering off from the Mini Ice Age, has been superstitious hysteria. The Veejack religion's adherents, encouraged by social media and political and academic elites hoping to overthrow the current social order, no longer blame the weather on witches, but instead blame it on the hydrocarbon fuel industry.[328] The Veejack religion's weather hysteria completely ignores the phenomenon that meteorologists refer to as

---

average in the twentieth century. The current warming trends are the easing of the grip of the Mini Ice Age.

[323] Blom, 225.

[324] Blom, 35, 128.

[325] Blom, 35.

[326] Blum, 251. Some scientists believe the weather was impacted by a volcano and point to the eruption of Mount Tambora in Indonesia in April 1815 as the cause of the "year without a summer."

[327] Blom, 55.

[328] Earth's weather is impacted by the angle of the sun; the rotation of the earth, the orbit of the earth; gravity of the earth, planets, and sun; the oceans and their currents; islands; mountain ranges; land masses; air pressure; and myriad other factors.

the Intertropical Convergence Zone (ITCZ). Brittanica describes the ITCZ as the:

> belt of converging trade winds and rising air that encircles Earth's lower atmosphere near the Equator. The rising air produces high cloudiness, frequent thunderstorms, and heavy rainfall; the doldrums, oceanic regions of calm surface air, also occur within the zone. The ITCZ shifts north and south seasonally with the Sun. Over the Indian Ocean, it undergoes especially large seasonal shifts of 40°–45° of latitude. Other large seasonal shifts in the position of the ITCZ occur over the eastern Pacific Ocean, South America, and Africa. The ITCZ plays a substantial role in slowing the mixing of air between Earth's Northern and Southern hemispheres (see also chemical equator).
>
> Aloft, air moving away from the ITCZ is an important factor in atmospheric circulation. As air descends in the subtropical high-pressure belts near latitudes 30° N and 30° S (the horse latitudes), it causes the trade winds to blow westward and equatorward at Earth's surface. These merge and rise in the ITCZ near the Equator and blow eastward and poleward at altitudes of 2 to 17 km (1 to 11 miles). Part of this flow descends in the subtropical high-pressure belts, and the remainder merges at high altitudes with the midlatitude westerly winds farther poleward. Precipitation generated within the ITCZ is a significant climatic control in several of Earth's tropical climate zones, particularly the wet equatorial climate, tropical wet-dry climate, the tropical monsoon and trade-wind littoral climate,

and the tropical and subtropical steppe climate (see also Köppen climate classification).[329]

The Veejack religious leaders' homilies denigrate those who use the capability of petroleum, natural gas, and coal capacity to fuel power plants, automobiles, and other land and seaborne transportation vehicles. The Veejack religious leaders blame the users of hydrocarbons for all unusual fluctuations in the weather, despite the historical data that fluctuations in weather are a normal recurring phenomenon. Historical data also shows a correlation between the "toxic combination of severe weather and fear."[330] The Veejack religious practices simulate the pillaring of witches by hanging in effigy officials of companies that profit from the power of hydrocarbons.

The proponents of the Veejack religion have also excitedly claimed that the oceans are rising and that island peoples will be overcome by the sea and their homes flooded. Even though as far back as 2021 an analysis of satellite imagery showed that Pacific Islands are actually growing, rather than shrinking, the Veejack religion is nevertheless preaching that low-lying islands are in danger.[331] An article in Hakai Magazine states:

> Though the sea level is rising, in the South Pacific, many low-lying islands are actually growing. Two studies published this year by the same team of researchers show that islands in the Federated States of Micronesia and the Gilbert Islands in the Republic of Kiribati have expanded their areas since the 1940s. The research is the latest in a line of

---

[329] https://www.britannica.com/science/intertropical-convergence-zone
[330] Blom, 59, 61.
[331] See, e.g., Besl, J., "The Ever-Shifting—Not Necessarily Shrinking—Pacific Island Nations", September 22, 2021, Hakai Magazine at https://hakaimagazine.com/news/the-ever-shifting-not-necessarily-shrinking-pacific-island-nations/

studies demonstrating that not all low-lying islands are doomed to drown.

In both studies, geomorphologists compared aerial reconnaissance photos captured during the Second World War with current satellite imagery. They ruled out landforms obscured by clouds or captured in low-resolution, as well as modified urban atolls like Tarawa, where half the population of Kiribati resides. In total, the scientists mapped 175 sparsely populated or entirely uninhabited islands, and compared how each had shifted, stretched, rotated, and sometimes shrunk over the past several decades.

The team found that while some islands shrank, plenty more expanded.[332]

In 2024 the New York Times headlined "The Vanishing Islands that Failed to Vanish," revealing that low-lying tropical island nations were prophesied to be victims of rising seas.[333] Raymond Zhong writing about the Maldives, tropical islands in the Indian Ocean, explains that ". . . when the world began paying attention to global warming decades ago, these islands, which form atop coral

---

[332] Besl, J. See, also, Faa, Marian, "Hundreds of Pacific Islands are getting bigger despite global warming", January 7, 2021, News – Pacific Beat at https://www.abc.net.au/news/2021-01-08/why-are-hundreds-of-pacific-islands-getting-bigger/13038430 writing "Scientists at the University of Auckland found atolls in the Pacific nations of Marshall Islands and Kiribati, as well as the Maldives archipelago in the Indian Ocean, have grown up to 8 per cent in size over the past six decades despite sea level rise"; and, *contra*, see, Arnall, Alex, "The Maldives is threatened by rising seas – but coastal development is causing even more pressing environmental issues", October 27, 2021, The Conversation at https://theconversation.com/the-maldives-is-threatened-by-rising-seas-but-coastal-development-is-causing-even-more-pressing-environmental-issues-170144.

[333] Zhong, Raymond and Gulley, Jason "The Vanishing Islands that Failed to Vanish", June 26, 2024, New York Times at https://www.nytimes.com/2024/06/27/briefing/maldives-atolls-climate-change.html

reefs in clusters called atolls, were quickly identified as some of the first places climate change might ravage in their entirety."[334] Zhong noted that although climate change enthusiasts had predicted the Maldives and other islands would be lost under the sea, a different pattern emerged. Zhong notes that researchers, after viewing data on close to one thousand islands, found otherwise. The researchers found that ". . . over the last few decades, the islands' edges had wobbled this way and that, eroding here, building there. By and large, though, their area hadn't shrunk. In some cases, it was the opposite: they grew. The seas rose, and the islands expanded with them."[335] The Veejack religion, however, does not publicize this data and continues to expect its adherents to fear the shibboleth of global warming/climate change and kowtow to the mantra of "bad carbon". In fact, most if not all of the Veejack religion's negative prophesies about hydrocarbons are misleading or outright falsehoods.

The Veejack religion ignores the reality of harnessing earth, air, water, and fire for the benefit of humankind. And the Veejack faith uses superstition, false science, fear, and propaganda for the political and economic benefit of the Veejack faith's elites.[336] By exciting dark weather and climate fantasies of doom and destruction in their followers, the Veejack religious elites in politics, industry, and public education gain political power and economic wealth. One of the Veejack religion's most insidious practices is to force conformity among academic and research meteorologists through the coercion

---

[334] Zhong, Raymond and Gulley, Jason.

[335] Zhong, Raymond and Gulley, Jason.

[336] An example of Veejack elites profiting from false science and propagandizing fear is the green-energy industrial complex (GEIC). The GEIC is composed of politically well-connected Veejack elites to whom the government funnels billions of dollars for products that are not profitable and are often not even brought to market. Nonetheless, the "executives" who run the GEIC are handsomely paid even as their companies go bankrupt. See, e.g., Moore, Stephen, "The biggest corporate welfare scam ever is green – Never forget, a lot of people are getting really, really rich off climate change hysteria and President Biden is helping them do it," April 10, 2024 at https://www.foxnews.com/opinion/biggest-corporate-welfare-scam-green

of withholding grant and scholarship funding. In short, the Veejack faith's political, economic, and educational elites who control the dispersal of government and private funding ensure that the funding goes only to meteorologists and meteorological scholars whose work will support the Veejack religion's climate change and global warming scare tactics. The Veejack religion refuses to allow funding for, or publication of, research that shows that earth's warming is governed by historical trends and not by human activity. That weather patterns are ever changing is anathema to Veejack religious elites who want to use people's fear of their own actions to control their behavior.

The planet Earth is amazingly resilient with extraordinary abilities for self-healing and recuperation. Our planet has recovered from volcanic eruptions, meteor strikes, forest fires, and other catastrophic events without human intervention. An example that is little covered by academics or media is how rapidly and thoroughly the oceans recovered from the devastation of World War II. And, when it is covered, it is portrayed as a "ticking time bomb" or other equally scary designation.[337] Although more than 3,800 ships in the Pacific were sunk during World War II the waters have not suffered from the "thousands of tons of oil and an unknown quantity of bombs . . .."[338] The Chuuck Lagoon, formerly known as Truk Lagoon, is the biggest collection of sunken ships and aircraft in the world.[339] Formerly a Japanese naval base, the Lagoon "is now a world-renowned dive site, famed for its sunken armada of ships and aircraft."[340] It was not always so pristine. As explained by writer, Craig Ryan:

[337] Heaton, Thomas (Grantee), "'Ticking Ecological Time Bombs': Thousands of Sunken WWII Ships Rusting at Bottom of Pacific", Pulitzer Center, December 6, 2022, at https://pulitzercenter.org/stories/ticking-ecological-time-bombs-thousands-sunken-wwii-ships-rusting-bottom-pacific.
[338] Heaton.
[339] Ryan, Craig, "Truk Lagoon – The Biggest Graveyard Of Ships In The World", December 1, 2023, NavalHistoria, at https://navalhistoria.com/truk-lagoon/
[340] Ryan.

The most significant event in Chuuk Lagoon's World War II history was Operation Hailstone, executed by the United States Navy on February 17-18, 1944. Recognizing Truk Lagoon's importance to Japanese war efforts, the U.S. launched a massive surprise attack, involving carrier-based aircraft and surface ships. Over two days, U.S. forces conducted continuous air raids, resulting in the sinking of more than 40 Japanese naval and merchant vessels and the destruction of 275 aircraft.[341]

Chuuck Lagoon today is "one of the world's most extraordinary wreck diving locations. The lagoon's floor is a veritable underwater museum."[342] As divers and sports enthusiasts have discovered the destruction and spills occasioned by combat during World War II was cleansed by natural processes without human assistance. Although World War II ended more than seventy-five years ago, there has been little actual damage, so the mantra is to use scare tactics. As shown in one article, beautifully multicolored coral now covers the Japanese merchant ship Kashi Maru sunken in the Solomon Islands.[343]

A novel aspect of the Veejack religion's belief system, but not necessarily connected to its theology, is the institution of "Earth Day". Earth Day is celebrated on April 22 or the day that the vernal equinox occurs.[344] This celebration of Earth Day mirrors the Pagen

---

[341] Ryan.

[342] Ryan. See, also, Ryan, Craig, "USS Oriskany – The Aircraft Carrier that Became an Artificial Reef", October 3, 2023, NavalHistoria, at https://navalhistoria.com/uss-oriskany/; and Ryan, Craig, "SS Thistlegorm – A Divers Paradise,: September 26, 2023, NavalHistoria, at https://navalhistoria.com/ss-thistlegorm/#google_vignette

[343] Heaton.

[344] National Geographic at https://education.nationalgeographic.org/resource/earth-day/ explains that "Earth Day is an annual celebration that honors the achievements of the environmental movement and raises awareness of the need to protect Earth's natural resources for future generations. Earth Day is celebrated on April 22 in the

worship of the goddess Mother Earth.[345] A modern equivalent of the Pagen worship of Mother Earth is the Wicca religion.[346] However, Wicca has many forms and "there is no official, authoritative text laying out exactly how people who practice Wicca are supposed to think, (and) it's a bit dicey to be generalizing about Wiccan beliefs".[347]

Earth Day is a direct challenge to Judeo-Christian beliefs that God created the earth.[348] One even hears Veejack religious followers greeting each other on April 22 each year with cries of "Happy Earth Day", which mimics and mocks the Judeo-Christian greetings of "Happy Hanukkah" and "Merry Christmas". In another challenge to Judeo-Christian traditions Earth Day occurs on the same day as the Judeo-Christian celebration of Passover.[349] The doctrine of

---

United States and on either April 22 or the day the spring equinox occurs throughout the rest of the world."

[345] As described on Wikipedia at https://en.wikipedia.org/wiki/Mother_goddess "A mother goddess is a major goddess characterized as a mother or progenitor, either as an embodiment of motherhood and fertility or fulfilling the cosmological role of a creator- and/or destroyer-figure, typically associated the Earth, sky, and/or the life-giving bounties thereof in a maternal relation with humanity or other gods. When equated in this lattermost function with the earth or the natural world, such goddesses are sometimes referred to as the Mother Earth or Earth Mother, deity in various animistic or pantheistic religions."

[346] Wikipedia at https://en.wikipedia.org/wiki/Wicca describes it thusly: " Wicca, also known as "The Craft", is a modern pagan, syncretic, earth-centered religion. Considered a new religious movement by scholars of religion, the path evolved from Western esotericism . . .."

[347] See, e.g., https://wiccaliving.com/essentials-wicca/

[348] See, Genesis 1:1-3 "In the beginning when God created the heavens and the earth, the earth was a formless void and darkness covered the face of the deep, while a wind from God swept over the face of the waters. Then God said, "Let there be light"; and there was light."

[349] Passover, is a major holiday for Rabbinical Judaism, Karaite Judaism, and Samaritanism that celebrates the Exodus of the Israelites from slavery in Biblical Egypt. Passover starts on the 15th day of the Hebrew month of Nisan, which is considered the first month of the Hebrew year. In 2024 Passover is celebrated on April 22. See, e.g., https://www.britannica.com/topic/Passover and https://en.wikipedia.org/wiki/Passover

the Earth Day organization conflates climate change with daily activities. Climate change, as discussed later, is controlled by forces including the sun, the gravity of other planets, earth's orbital plane and earth's axial position. Earth Day's website includes a flawed description of climate that includes almost all human activity to the complete exclusion of scientifically accepted causes, such as the Milankovitch cycles that are discussed below. Earth Day's website describes it this way:

> Climate education is cross-cutting by nature, meaning it encompasses many topics like math, civics, economics and history. Similarly, all aspects of our daily lives are connected to climate — from the food we eat, to the way we travel to work, to the products we buy. The inter connectedness of the systems involved in climate change amplifies the need for environmental and climate education to include concepts outside of STEM (science, technology, engineering and math) like the arts, English, economics and history. Individuals connect to the environment in different ways depending on their own individual identities based on how they live, where they were raised, and what fields of study they choose for their careers.[350]

The Veejack religion's views on climate echo the views of primitive religions throughout history that persuaded their followers to do their bidding because the elites told them that their behavior impacted the environment. The elites often alleged that the peoples' behavior was the reason for naturally occurring events such as plagues of locusts or rabbits eating the crops, abnormal weather including excessive heat or cold, unseasonable drought or rain, dust in the air,

---

[350] See, Earth Day website at https://www.earthday.org/wp-content/uploads/2024/04/Climate-Education-vs-The-Climate-Crisis.pdf

forest fires, etc.[351] In every case, the elites used naturally occurring events to justify their desired political or economic ends. The elites, who are better educated than most of the populace, know that the weather is always changing, that locusts and rabbits come and go, and today's catastrophe will soon be overtaken by tomorrow's new catastrophe. In this way the elites continually manipulate the populace for their own ends.

Weather and climate are distinctly different. Climate change occurs over millennia, while weather patterns change from year to year, decade to decade, and century to century; and are therefore measurable in the near term. For example, while recent centuries have shown slightly warmer temperatures, this warming has occurred previously. In fact, the cyclical changes between warm and cold weather patterns have shaped history for thousands of years.

Climate changes over millennia due to forces external to the earth, as well as by immediate impact caused by volcanoes, shifting ocean currents, glacial melting, and meteorites. Astronomer, mathematician, and climatologist Milutin Milanković explained that long-term climate variations on Earth are caused by the position of the Earth in comparison to the Sun.[352] These cycles include the earth's tilt as it rotates on its axis, whether the earth's orbit around the sun is more circular or elliptical, and the pull of gravity on earth exerted by other planets as they rotate around the sun. These cycles

---

[351] Blaming naturally occurring events on "climate change" is a favorite tactic. The most ridiculous claims include blaming an earthquake (see, Hays, Gabriel, "U.S. Senate candidate goes viral for blaming NY earthquake on climate change, deletes post – Congressman Dan Crenshaw, R-Texas, marveled, 'I was just joking about people blaming climate change and then this genius pops up'," April 6, 2024 at https://www.foxnews.com/media/u-s-senate-candidate-viral-blaming-ny-earthquake-climate-change-deletes-post); blaming climate change for cicadas, solar eclipse, and earthquake (See, Hunter, Heather, "Sunny Hostin speculates cicadas, solar eclipse, and earthquake could be caused by 'climate change'," April 9, 2024 at https://www.msn.com/en-us/tv/news/sunny-hostin-speculates-cicadas-solar-eclipse-and-earthquake-could-be-caused-by-climate-change/ar-BB1lhyje);
[352] See, Milutin Milanković at https://en.wikipedia.org/wiki/Milutin_Milankovic

are known as Milankovitch cycles.[353] The earth alternates between ice ages and more temperate climates. Thankfully for the unfolding of man's intellect and cultural advancement the earth is currently in an interglacial period.[354]

There are many astonishing examples of real climate change, rather than the ordinary weather changes that are preached by the Veejack faith as "climate change". One example of real climate change involves North Africa. Surprisingly, what is now the Sahara Desert has periodically been vast well-watered savannahs with rivers, lakes, and verdant grasslands. As Edward Armstrong, a Postdoctoral Research Fellow at the University of Helsinki, writes, approximately 6,000 to 11,000 years ago the Sahara was "a vibrant savannah inhabited by elephants, giraffes, rhinos and hippos."[355] Scientists refer to this period as the Green Sahara or North African Humid Period.[356] Armstrong explains that there is "widespread climatological evidence that during this period the Sahara supported wooded savannah ecosystems and numerous rivers and lakes in what are now Libya, Niger, Chad and Mali."[357]

---

[353] See, https://en.wikipedia.org/wiki/Milankovitch_cycles

[354] See, https://en.wikipedia.org/wiki/Interglacial that explains that "an interglacial period (or alternatively interglacial, interglaciation) is a geological interval of warmer global average temperature lasting thousands of years that separates consecutive glacial periods within an ice age. (Earth's) current Holocene interglacial began at the end of the Pleistocene, about 11,700 years ago."

[355] Armstrong, Edward, "The Sahara Desert used to be a green savannah – new research explains why," December 15, 2023, The Conversation at https://theconversation.com/the-sahara-desert-used-to-be-a-green-savannah-new-research-explains-why-216555, published in *Nature Communications*. See, also, "New research reveals why and when the Sahara Desert was green," University of Bristol, December 13, 2023, at https://phys.org/news/2023-09-reveals-sahara-green.html#:~:text=Lead%20author%20Dr.%20Edward%20Armstrong%2C%20a%20climate%20scientist,the%20most%20remarkable%20environmental%20changes%20on%20the%20planet.%22

[356] Armstrong.

[357] Armstrong.

As with most climate fluctuations, the pattern of desert and greening in North Africa is repetitive. The Sahara turns green approximately every 21,000 years. By reviewing marine and lake sediments, Armstrong writes that "scientists have identified over 230 of these greenings . . . over the past eight million years. These greening events provided vegetated corridors which influenced species' distribution and evolution, including the out-of-Africa migrations of ancient humans."[358] The cause of the repetitive desert-to-green cycle required a "large-scale reorganization of the atmospheric system to bring rains to this hyper arid region" and has been identified as "caused by changes in the Earth's orbital precession - the slight wobbling of the planet while rotating. This moves the Northern Hemisphere closer to the sun during the summer months."[359] There are many benefits to the earth from this cycle. Currently, with the Sahara in the desert part of the cycle, its dust is carried by strong winds to replenish the phosphorus in the Amazon rain forest.[360]

Having hypothesized that climate change is caused by "variations

---

[358] Armstrong.

[359] Armstrong.

[360] See, e.g., https://www.nasa.gov/centers-and-facilities/goddard/nasa-satellite-reveals-how-much-saharan-dust-feeds-amazons-plants/ which describes the process as follows:

> The Sahara Desert is a near-uninterrupted brown band of sand and scrub across the northern third of Africa. The Amazon rain forest is a dense green mass of humid jungle that covers northeast South America. But after strong winds sweep across the Sahara, a tan cloud rises in the air, stretches between the continents, and ties together the desert and the jungle. It's dust. And lots of it.
>
> For the first time, a NASA satellite has quantified in three dimensions how much dust makes this trans-Atlantic journey. Scientists have not only measured the volume of dust, they have also calculated how much phosphorus – remnant in Saharan sands from part of the desert's past as a lake bed – gets carried across the ocean from one of the planet's most desolate places to one of its most fertile.

***** ***** *****

in the earth's orbit" Armstrong shows other non-human factors that influence the earth's orbit and climate change. He writes:

> Due to gravitational influences from the moon and other planets in our solar system, the orbit of the Earth around the sun is not constant. It has cyclic variations on multi-thousand-year timescales. These orbital cycles are termed Milankovitch cycles; they influence the amount of energy the Earth receives from the sun.[361]

Notwithstanding Armstrong's now widely accepted hypothesis on the impact of the earth's axis wobble on climate change, other writers persist in trying to peg the desert and greening cycles to human activity. In 2017, prior to Armstrong publishing his theory, it was argued that human activity was to blame for the most recent desertification of the Sahara.[362] Archaeologist David Wright wrote that "maybe humans and their goats tipped the balance".[363] His theory is that every time there occurs:

> the presence of "pastoralists"—humans with their domesticated animals—there was a corresponding

---

Specifically the dust picked up from the Bodélé Depression in Chad, an ancient lake bed where rock minerals composed of dead microorganisms are loaded with phosphorus. Phosphorus is an essential nutrient for plant proteins and growth, which the Amazon rain forest depends on in order to flourish.

[361] Armstrong.

[362] Wright, David K., "Humans as Agents in the Termination of the African Humid Period," January 26, 2017, Frontiers, in Earth Science, 1-14. See, also, Boissoneault, Lorraine, "What Really Turned the Sahara Desert From a Green Oasis Into a Wasteland? - 10,000 years ago, this iconic desert was unrecognizable. A new hypothesis suggests that humans may have tipped the balance", March 24, 2017, Smithsonian Magazine at https://www.smithsonianmag.com/science-nature/what-really-turned-sahara-desert-green-oasis-wasteland-180962668/

[363] Boissoneault.

change in the types and variety of plants. It was as if, every time humans and their goats and cattle hopscotched across the grasslands, they had turned everything to scrub and desert in their wake.[364]

This far-fetched attempt to blame human activity for normal weather patterns is just one of many attempts to discount the perceptiveness of Armstrong's theory. It is another attempt to persuade the susceptible and gullible to follow the Veejack religious elites and help fund their political and economic goals.

A most vivid example of an impact on weather is the six-mile-wide asteroid that struck Mexico's Yucatan Peninsula 170 million years ago killing off the dinosaurs and ending the Cretaceous age.[365] In addition to ending the reign of the dinosaurs, the impact of the immense asteroid wiped out "75 percent of known species" on earth.[366]

It is the weather that impacts human activity and not human activity that impacts the weather. A spectacular impact of changing weather on human activity is the fall of the Roman Empire. After ruling Western Europe, North Africa, and lands east of the Mediterranean Sea for more than half a millennium, the Empire collapsed. Stanford University's Ian Morris' universal social-development index, reveals that the fall of Rome was the greatest setback in the history of human civilization.[367] Many modern historians now trace the fall of the Roman

---

[364] Boissoneault.

[365] Black, Riley, "What Happened in the Seconds, Hours, Weeks After the Dino-Killing Asteroid Hit Earth? – The Cretaceous forecast: Tsunamis, a deadly heat pulse, and massive cooling," August 9, 2016, Smithsonian Magazine at https://www.smithsonianmag.com/science-nature/dinosaur-killing-asteroid-impact-chicxulub-crater-timeline-destruction-180973075/

[366] Black.

[367] Kyle Harper, Aeon, "How Climate Change and Plague Helped Bring Down the Roman Empire – We can learn crucial lessons by examining the natural forces that shaped Rome's rise and fall", December 19, 2017, Smithsonian Magazine at https://www.smithsonianmag.com/science-nature/how-climate-change-and-disease-helped-fall-rome-180967591/

Empire to a cyclical weather pattern that turned Europe cold.[368] It was not internal political feuding that fragmented the once-glorious Empire, but instead it was the natural environment and "the inherent unpredictability of nature."[369] Regarding whether climate change is a modern phenomenon, Smithsonian Magazine points out that:

> climate change did not begin with the exhaust fumes of industrialization, but has been a permanent feature of human existence. Orbital mechanics (small variations in the tilt, spin and eccentricity of the Earth's orbit) and solar cycles alter the amount and distribution of energy received from the Sun. And volcanic eruptions spew reflective sulphates into the atmosphere, sometimes with long-reaching effects.[370]

Weather may have also generated the prosperity of the Roman Empire. During its epoch, the Mediterranean and surrounding areas largely agrarian culture had warm, wet, and stable weather that created economic prosperity.[371] The Empire's prosperity ended when "an enormous spasm of volcanic activity in the 530s and 540s" occurred and "triggered what is now called the 'Late Antique Little Ice Age,' when much colder temperatures endured for at least 150 years."[372]

More recently, the "Medieval Warm Period" also known as the "Medieval Climate Optimum" or the "Medieval Climatic Anomaly," was a time of warm climate in the North Atlantic region that lasted

---

[368] Kyle Harper, Aeon, "How Climate Change and Plague Helped Bring Down the Roman Empire – We can learn crucial lessons by examining the natural forces that shaped Rome's rise and fall", December 19, 2017, Smithsonian Magazine at https://www.smithsonianmag.com/science-nature/how-climate-change-and-disease-helped-fall-rome-180967591/

[369] Harper.

[370] Harper.

[371] Harper.

[372] Harper.

from c. 950 to c. 1250."[373] And this warm period was followed by "a regionally cooler period in the North Atlantic and elsewhere, which is sometimes called the Little Ice Age (LIA)."[374]

The cold periods have occurred at other times as well. In recent centuries there have been three cold intervals, as "one began about 1650, another about 1770, and the last in 1850, all of which were separated by intervals of slight warming."[375] Much like the Veejack religion's tactic of blaming weather patterns on human activity, during the Little Ice Age European leaders blamed the cold weather on evil witches and hundreds were burned or killed in other ways.[376] The fact that the earth is now warming incrementally from year to year is not the result of human activity, it is because the earth is still emerging from the last little ice age.

The Veejack faith uses unsupported pseudo-science and unproveable hypothesis that project catastrophes occurring in the distant future to play on its supporters' emotions and coerce them into engaging in disadvantageous economic and political behaviors. One of the Veejack religion's favorite tales is that rising levels of carbon dioxide is causing the earth's temperature to rise.[377] Other research reported in *The Western Journal*, [378] however, found that rising temperatures on earth are caused by the sun. In an article *The Western Journal* reported the opinion of multiple solar physics and climate science experts that "solar energy is more of a cause for global warming than carbon dioxide."[379] This opinion was

---

[373] https://en.wikipedia.org/wiki/Medieval_Warm_Period

[374] *Id.*

[375] https://en.wikipedia.org/wiki/Little_Ice_Age.

[376] Blom, 58.

[377] Human Events Staff, "Study Finds Sun May Be Leading Cause of Global Warming," August 26, 2021, at https://humanevents.com/2021/08/26/study-finds-sun-may-be-leading-cause-of-global-warming/

[378] Please note that Wikipedia https://en.wikipedia.org/wiki/The_Western_Journal at writes that "*The Western Journal* . . . is an American conservative news and politics website . . .."

[379] Human Events Staff, "Study Finds Sun May Be Leading Cause of Global Warming," August 26, 2021, at https://humanevents.com/2021/08/26/

attacked by the "experts" that support the carbon monoxide theory. Notwithstanding the need for open and free intellectual debate on the causes of earth's warming, the study that appeared in *The Western Journal* was retracted after the "carbon monoxide" scientists, worried that their theory was challenged by even one source, browbeat the *Journal* into retracting the article.[380]

By citing actual environmental problems involving temporarily polluted air, water, or soil the Veejack religion's elites portray them as "proof" of the "truth" of dire future horrors. These dire future horrors can only be prevented, the Veejack religion's elites state, by performing penance in their daily lives and economic choices. Instead of purchasing cost-effective gas-powered automobiles they must use expensive and inefficient electric vehicles. Instead of making tasty and healthy food choices they must eat bland vegetable-derived chemical creations that taste like cardboard. Instead of worshipping the God of Abraham they must pay obeisance to unnamed gods that control the weather and inflict floods, drought, pestilence, and abnormal temperatures on those who dare to defy the Veejack religion's elites.

The most potent weapon in the Veejack religion's arsenal for coercing behavior in their followers is personal ridicule. The Veejack religion's elites are skilled at using group psychosis and heard instincts as they hurl volleys of insults at their opponents. The volume and intensity at which the Veejack religion's elites launch invective at their opponents reflects the degree of accuracy in the opponent's argument and the fear by the Veejack faithful of loss of influence if the argument is believed. Regarding weather, the favorite Veejack religious tactic is to label dissenters as "climate deniers" when, instead, the opposing voice is more likely a "weather realist."

The Veejack faith's favorite technique for terrorizing its followers is to take naturally occurring events, portray them as uniquely

---

study-finds-sun-may-be-leading-cause-of-global-warming/.

[380] See, https://www.westernjournal.com/study-nearly-2-dozen-scientists-finds-sun-not-co2-may-chief-cause-global-warming/.

the fault of human activity, and use them to justify funding for their political and economic benefit. For example, if the weather is abnormally cold, it is the fault of the populace for burning fossil fuel and blocking the sun so its heat cannot reach the surface. Yet if the weather is abnormally hot it is also the fault of the populace for burning fossil fuel because the effect is to trap greenhouse gases so the heat cannot radiate out into space. In their effort to propagandize their followers the Veejack religious elites only concentrate on local weather, without disclosing world weather patterns. When the United States is abnormally warm, as occurred recently, the Veejack religious elites failed to inform its followers that the weather in Europe and Asia was abnormally frigid. Similarly, if blizzards afflict the United States while heatwaves leave Europe and Asia sweltering it is only the blizzards that are mentioned by the Veejack religion's elites. As the National Air and Space Agency (NASA) points out, "exceptionally cold winters in one place might be balanced by extremely warm winters in another part of the world."[381]

The earliest recorded religious texts, including the ancient Mesopotamian story of Atrahasis, Enuma Elish, and the Epic of Gilgamesh had gods who were created by or controlled elements of the weather including the sky, earth, waters, thunder and lightning and sent floods to punish people.[382] Within the Gilgamesh epic, Ishtar was the goddess of thunderstorms and rain.[383] In the religion in Canaan, in modern day Israel, "when (the Canaanite god) Baal dies, there is no rain. The wadis dry up and the fields are dry. When he comes back to life the rain comes again."[384]

Within the Canaanite religion curses were placed on nature to prevent rain.[385] In ancient Egypt the primary god was the sun-god

---

[381] https://earthobservatory.nasa.gov/world-of-change/global-temperatures.
[382] Collins, 32-40.
[383] Collins, 40.
[384] Collins, 55.
[385] Collins, 45.

Re.[386] And the most famous instance of God impacting the weather is the story of Noah, who was famously warned by God to build an ark and save his family and animals.[387] Justinian, the 6th century Emperor of the Eastern Roman Empire, believed homosexuality was a cause of natural disasters.[388] Catholic Saint Hildegard of Bingen, an 11th century nun, theologian, composer, author and mystic believed that human behavior affects the world's climate; that "sin creates adverse weather conditions which in turn leads to plagues and blights, producing an earthly Purgatory by a process that is at once divine judgement and natural law."[389]

And the religions that worshipped weather gods, from the ancient Canaanite Ba'al and Egyptian Horus; to the Norse-Germanic Thor and Greco-Roman Jupiter, Tempestas and Zeus;

---

[386] Collins, 47. Also, as Collins notes at 49, "the God of Israel is sometimes described with solar imagery . . .."

[387] Genesis, chapters 5-9. The story of Noah is also told in the Islamic Koran (Surahs 71, 7, 11, 54, 21).

[388] David F. Greenberg and Marcia H. Bystryn, "Christian Intolerance of Homosexuality", *American Journal of Sociology*, 88, No. 3 (1982), pp. 515-548, 530. See, also, Stamps, Robert F. (2022) "Christians Must Reach Out to the Oppressed " Loyola Marymount University, *Say Something Theological: The Student Journal of Theological Studies*: Vol. 5: Iss. 1, Article 10.

[389] Barbara Newman, Hildegard of Bingen and the "Birth of Purgatory', *Mystics Quarterly*, 19 No. 3, 1993, 90-97, 93. That sin may affect climate change is described in Hildegard's writing, *Causae et Curae*, found at http://home.kpn.nl/i.w.c.emmens/pdf/causcur.pdf. A passage in Book 2, section 124, at pages 35-36 and reads:

Revenge of God. If at any time by God's judgment the elements project their terrors in a chaotic way, they inflict many dangers on the world and men. And is that the fire is like a spear, the wind like a sword, water as a shield and earth like a javelin called to punish men. For the elements are subordinate to man and as they concern the actions of men, so fulfill their own duty. Indeed, when men engage in battles, catastrophes, hatred, envy, and improper sins, then the elements behave differently and adversely in regard to heat, cold, heavy rains, or floods.

And this is so according to the first disposition of God, which established that the elements behave according to the works of men, that affect the actions of men and that man acts in them and with them. When men are on the right track and do the good and the bad in moderation, then the elements do their duty by the grace of God according to the needs of men.

the Hindu-Vedic Indra and Mariamman; and the numerous Maya, Taino and Aztec weather gods show that religions from the earliest times have used human impact on weather events to require rituals and exact offerings from the people.[390] The Veejack faith has adopted and proclaims the belief that human behavior alters weather and climate. The Veejack religion garbs its primitive religious tenant that human behavior impacts the weather in the flashy cloths of science and the unproven – and unproveable – theories of meteorologists and climatologists. The Veejack religion's theoreticians pretend that ordinary weather patterns are evidence of climate change,[391] however that does not change this religious belief into secularism. The Veejack faith's doctrine on climate and weather differs markedly from acceptable scientific proof that unchecked carbon output may put toxins into the nearby land, waters and atmosphere; however, to exact ritual abstinence and taxes based on visions of carbon-induced harm in the distant future – even though firmly believed by its adherents – are no different than the beliefs of Justinian and Hildegard that their concepts of sin impacted the weather and those of more primitive religions that worshipped weather gods through the ages.

---

[390] See, e.g., https://en.wikipedia.org/wiki/Weather_god and https://stormguardrc.com/the-history-of-weather-gods/

[391] "Climate change" is Veejack's catch-all phrase to underpin its various demands impacting petroleum products, solar and wind farms, transportation, forest management, water rights and usage, home heating, farming, raising livestock, and many other areas of commerce that it seeks to regulate and/or tax.

CHAPTER EIGHT

VEEJACK RELIGION INVENTS LAWFARE

Marginalizing and Subjugating Rural People

The Veejack religion and its allies have manipulated the United States legal system as an openly visible, but uniquely stealthy, strategy to further its authoritarian movement's goals. The leaders of the Veejack religion recognize that there is a dichotomy between urban and rural peoples, with rural and agricultural people less inclined to accept the Veejack religion or its theology of authoritarian rule. Beginning with the early twentieth century Progressive Movement, and gaining steam in the 1930s, the Veejack religion began to transform the United States. One of the Veejack religion's goals was to marginalize rural and agricultural people, who were most resistant to the Veejack religion's theologies, and to consolidate authority within the major urban centers. A key diminution of rural political power began with the adoption of the Seventeenth Amendment to the United States Constitution, which mandated majoritarian election of United States Senators.[392]

---

[392] U.S. Const. Art. l, §3, cl. 1, amended 1919 (U.S. Const. Amend. XVII).

Prior to the adoption of the Seventeenth Amendment, many United States Senators were selected by the state's legislature. Many state legislatures had one body of the legislature elected by majoritarian voting, and the other body of the legislature was based on geographic distribution. Thus, if for example, in one body of the legislature each county had equal representation, then the rural counties would tend to control that body of the legislature.[393] This format provided rural and agricultural people with not only a strong voice in state government, but a voice in the selection of United States Senators.

However, after enactment of the Seventeenth Amendment and other Progressive manipulation, the political power of rural and agricultural people began to wane. In the 1930s the Veejack religion gained ascendancy as President Franklin Roosevelt, frustrated at the Supreme Court for judicially blocking many of his New Deal attempts to transform the political balance within the United States, cowed it into submission.[394] Throughout the previous history of the United States in a system referred to as Federalism, political power was shared between the individual States and the Federal government.[395] Under Federalism, the individual States had unique powers, and the Federal government could not intrude on those powers. Roosevelt, as a leader in imposing Veejack religious theology, sought to use the judicial system to further the transformation of the balance of power between urban and rural people. Under Roosevelt the Federal government appropriated authority that was previously resident in the States and transferred it to the Federal government.

---

[393] See, e.g., *Gray v. Sanders*, 372 U.S. 368 (1963) for an example of a state, Georgia, which had representation by county.

[394] See, e.g., "Judicial Procedures Reform Bill of 1937" at https://en.wikipedia.org/wiki/Judicial_Procedures_Reform_Bill_of_1937.

[395] For an understanding of the founder's theories of government, see, e.g., Hamilton, Alexander, Madison, James, Rossiter, Clinton, Jay, John, and Kesler, Charles R., *The Federalist Papers*, New York: Signet Classics, an Imprint of New American Library, a Division of Penguin Group (USA), 2005.

One of the practices of the Veejack religion was to use a tactic now known as "lawfare".[396]

The premise of lawfare is simple: use Federal Judges and Appeals Courts to support previously unconstitutional legislation by eviscerating previous judicial and legislative traditions that were contrary to the theologies and philosophy of the Veejack religion. Through lawfare the Veejack religion uses the legal system to impose policies it is unable to obtain through legislation.

While there were many pernicious examples of the Veejack religion's use of lawfare to achieve its goals, the most consequential and possibly the worst decision of the United States Supreme Court in the twentieth century was *Reynolds v. Sims*, 377 U.S. 533 (1964).[397] The *Reynolds* decision achieved the Veejack religion's objective of marginalizing rural people and subjugating them to the domination of the urban elites. Prior to the decision in *Reynolds* the makeup of individual state legislatures mirrored the legislatures of the United States Federal government. The Federal government has a House of Representatives whose members are apportioned based on population.[398] The Federal government also has a legislative chamber known as the Senate. The Senate is not based on population, but each state, no matter how small, has two Senators.[399] Prior to the *Reynolds* decision many individual states had a legislative chamber based on population, like the Federal House of Representatives, and also had a legislative chamber based on geographic boundaries that was

---

[396] Beginning in the 2020s, the Veejack religion's elites adapted "lawfare" to the criminal justice system by using criminal charges as a political weapon against its enemies.

[397] This case was derived from earlier rulings in *Baker v. Carr*, 369 U.S. 186 (1962) and *Gray v. Sanders*, 372 U.S. 368 (1963).

[398] U S Const. Art 1, §2. This section states "Representatives . . . shall be apportioned among the several States which may be included within this Union, according to their respective Numbers . . . ."

[399] U S Const. Art 1, §3. This section states "(t)he Senate of the United States shall be composed of two Senators from each State, chosen by the Legislature thereof, for six Years; and each Senator shall have one Vote."

similar to the Federal Senate. The state boundaries for geographic representation recognized that urban, suburban, exurban, rural, and agricultural people have different views, needs, and goals.

Mistakenly applying the Fourteenth Amendment's principle of "one person, one vote", *Reynolds* eviscerated the equalizing value of the dynamic tension between urban and suburban, exurban, rural, and agricultural voters and transferred all legislative power to the densely populated urban areas.[400] The "one person, one vote" scenario is mistakenly derived from the language of the Fourteenth Amendment to the Constitution which reads, in part, "No State shall make or enforce any law which shall abridge the privileges or immunities of citizens of the United States; nor shall any State deprive any person of life, liberty, or property, without due process of law; nor deny to any person within its jurisdiction the equal protection of the laws".[401]

Prior to *Reynolds,* representation in one of the state's legislative chambers was based on factors other than population, such as by county or other geographic factors. Before *Reynolds* the Supreme Court had denied a similar challenge, holding that the makeup of the State legislature was a nonjusticiable political question.[402] By emulating the Federal Senate, which assures that legislative power represents even less populated states, the pre-*Reynolds* apportionment ensured that rural areas' needs, beliefs, and values would be represented and respected in the various state legislatures.

---

[400] Urban areas have masses of people and large numbers of people on public assistance living in concentrated areas. Within the public assistance areas Veejack has appointed unofficial "block captains" to ensure voter turnout for Veejack-favored candidates. Many of these people do not follow politics and are unaware of the candidates and issues. Nevertheless, the Veejack block captains go door-to-door and often use veiled threats and intimidation to influence the peoples' selection of candidates. These methods help install Veejack believers in administrative, legislative, and judicial positions of power from which they can prompt adoption of their Veejack religious policies.

[401] U S Const. Amend. 16, §1.

[402] *Colegrove v. Green*, 328 U.S. 549 (1946).

At this point it is important to recognize the Veejack religion's goal is to destabilize both the urban and rural societies in the United States. In the cities and other urban areas where the people enjoyed parks, playgrounds, benches to relax and enjoy the outdoors, and other amenities the Veejack religion's policies were imposed by their political helpers and have upended people's daily routines and leisure activities. Using the COVID panic as an excuse to impose draconian dictatorial restrictions on public activity, the Veejack religion's elites delighted in controlling personal freedom. The Veejack religion's followers in government imposed social boundaries that were previously unknown: social distancing, shuttering restaurants and stores, closing schools, requiring telecommuting for almost all businesses, sparking panic buying of toilet paper and paper towels, stopping rapid transit, and countless other measures. The Veejack religion's elites also welcomed the mentally ill, substance abusers, and criminals to move into and dominate public spaces.

The Veejack religion hijacked the scenic parks, well maintained playgrounds, protected wetlands, and other areas where the public had enjoyed outdoor activity.[403] Benches, where previously the elderly could rest while walking, and mothers could relax and watch as their children played, were requisitioned as makeshift beds for the homeless, the mentally ill, or the inebriated. Pleasant spaces became unsafe or unavailable, where before the COVID chaos they contained platforms for the public to enjoy chess, checkers, and other games. The Veejack faithful imposed disorder on the public. Veejack religious elites, safe in their gated communities and guarded apartment complexes, demanded that the mentally ill, substance abusers, and criminals be allowed to live in public spaces.

---

[403] See, e.g., "RV encampment impacting the Ballona Freshwater Marsh", January 16, 2022, Spectrum News at https://spectrumnews1.com/ca/la-west/homelessness/2022/01/16/rv-encampment-is-impacting-the-ballona-freshwater-marsh; and "An Additional 1000 ft of RVs and Encampments Cleared at Ballona Wetlands", August 2, 2023, Westside Current at https://www.westsidecurrent.com/news/an-additional-1000-ft-of-rvs-and-encampments-cleared-at-ballona-wetlands/article_50de97cc-2cb4-11ee-8e94-4b430d1247d0.html.

These wretched derelicts who should have been institutionalized or incarcerated, were permitted to erect shelters, pitch tents and park decrepit campers and RVs, or just throw cardboard on the ground, in a kaleidoscope of horror resembling the worst of refugee camps. Judeo-Christian houses of worship were cajoled and guilted into offering their buildings and yards as camps for migrants and the desolate.[404]

Desperately needed care was denied to the mentally ill on the theory that desolate lives were actually a lifestyle choice. Mass transit ceased to provide a clean and comfortable transportation alternative. Instead, subways and buses became a challenging ordeal as paying passengers had to avoid the pitiful "stall jumpers" who brought crime, grime, and disease to the transportation system's carriages and buses. The nonpaying users often roared insults, slept, vomited, defecated, urinated, and used needles to inject drugs with no police interference. The Veejack religion fostered these horrors and cheered as the Veejack religion's attack on civilization began to rip the social fabric apart and destroy businesses, recreation, and churches.

Unlike people living in urban and suburban areas, the attacks on rural and agricultural peoples used a strategy based on regulating and taxing petroleum. Petroleum products, generally in the form of refillable fuel tanks, are used to heat rural houses, barns and outbuildings during the cold times. And, as rural and agricultural people do not have access to mass transit, they must travel long distances in petroleum fueled private vehicles to obtain food, clothing, furniture, health care and other necessities of life.

The Veejack religion and urban elites preach, as part of their faith, that gasoline and diesel-powered vehicles and heating are

---

[404] This process of abusing the hospitality of the Judeo-Christian houses of worship was exacerbated by President Biden's disastrous open-border policies that allowed millions of undocumented, unvaccinated, and unemployed people to drain Judeo-Christian resources. As the Judeo-Christian organizations tried to help the individual migrants the Veejack elites delighted in enacting policies that increased the rate of illegal border crossings until the pressure inundated and destroyed the congregations' and temples' capability to react and serve.

bad and even harmful.[405] The Veejack religious elites, who travel in chauffeured limousines and luxury taxis, have no idea of the cost they impose on rural and agricultural people by inflicting on them the high fuel taxes that cripple rural economies. If rural and agricultural people were adequately represented in one chamber of each state's legislature, they would have the power to ensure that their unique needs were met.

In the Supreme Court case of *Gray v. Sanders*[406] Justice William Orville "Bill" Douglas, an avowed progressive and radical creator of many of the evolving Veejack faith's theologies exposed his anti-rural bias.[407] Justice Douglas, who attended Columbia Law School and had previously been on the faculty at Yale Law School, delivered the opinion of the Court. Justice Douglas piously asked "(h)ow can one person be given . . . (greater) voting power (over) another person in a statewide election merely because he lives in a rural area or because he lives in the smallest rural county?"[408] Justice Douglas thereby tossed away the United States Founder's ideas, deeply embedded in the Constitution, that in the Senatorial chamber the smaller areas need equal representation with the highly populated areas. Justice Douglas ignored and eroded this concept of rural representation that was mirrored at the State level. Instead, he dumped it on the trash heap, disregarding "(t)he only weighting of votes sanctioned by the Constitution concerns matters of representation, such as the

---

[405] See, Chapter Seven "Climate and the Weather Gods".

[406] *Gray v. Sanders*, 372 U.S. 368 (1963).

[407] Time Magazine referred to Douglas as an "undeviating liberal", "a dangerous radical" and the "most doctrinaire and committed civil libertarian ever to sit on the court." Douglas did not rely on legal reasoning for his opinions on the Court. Instead, his untethered prose, bereft of logic helped plant the seeds that sprouted into Veejack. Although Douglas' impact on the Veejack faith is huge, Time noted that "his impact on the court was diminished by his failure to include the legal reasoning behind his opinions . . . (and failure to have) opinions with careful arguments will probably cause Douglas not to be ranked right at the top by the experts". See, "The Law: The Court's Uncompromising Libertarian". Time.com. November 24, 1975 at https://time.com/archive/6847475/the-law-the-courts-uncompromising-libertarian/

[408] *Gray v. Sanders*, 372 U.S. 368 (1963).

allocation of Senators irrespective of population . . .."[409] The Supreme Court demolishing State government representation of rural people is discreditable; and has resulted in the domination of exurban, rural, and agricultural people by city bosses and their cronies.[410]

After *Reynolds,* urban politicians dominated the state legislatures.[411] The urban representatives did not and do not respect the needs, beliefs, and values of their state's rural population. Surprisingly, the Court turned to the Fourteenth Amendment's Equal Protection Clause as the basis for its decision. The Court sarcastically noted that "legislators represent people, not trees or acres. Legislators are elected by voters, not farms or cities or economic interests."[412] However, the result was that the court condemned rural people to subjugation and established the domination of states by urban elites.[413]

---

[409] *Gray v. Sanders*, 372 U.S. 368, 380 (1963).

[410] As Chief Justice Earl Warren, like Justice Douglas an early creator of Veejack doctrine, wrote in *Reynolds v. Sims*, 377 U.S. 533, 562 (1964), "(a)s long as ours is a representative form of government, and our legislatures are those instruments of government elected directly by and directly representative of the people, the right to elect legislators in a free and unimpaired fashion is a bedrock of our political system." Without a hint of why the States had bicameral legislatures, which like the United States Congress, could represent multiple interests with one chamber elected by popular vote and the other representing the individual States, the Supreme Court crushed the rural and agricultural people and subjected them to domination by the urban elites, who are increasingly converting to the Veejack religion.

[411] As Chemerinsky points out, at 956, the Supreme Court "concluded that both houses of a state legislature must be apportioned by population. A state is not allowed to mirror Congress where the House is apportioned by population and Senate seats are allocated two to each state regardless of population."

[412] *Reynolds v. Sims*, 377 U.S. 533 (1964).

[413] The only exception to this rule is in the case of *Ball v. James*, 451 U.S. 355 (1981) where the Supreme Court held that a water storage district could permit a one-acre, one-vote rule; *contra*, see, e.g., Board of Estimates v. Morris, 489 U.S. 688 (1989), that prohibited deviation from the one-person, one-vote rule in election to New York City's Board of Estimates. Chemerinsky, at 959, correctly notes that the Court can be criticized for "excessive judicial activism because there was not authority in the text or the framer's intent for the rule of one-person, one-vote. The critics see the decisions as improper judicial interference, unsupported by the text of the Constitution or the

The Income Tax as an Example
of Wealth Discrimination

Although the *Reynolds* Court relied on the Fourteenth Amendment's Equal Protection Clause to discriminate against rural people, the Court has not used the Equal Protection Clause to protect working people from excessive taxation on their income. Prior to the early 20th century, the Federal government had no authority to impose a Federal income tax.[414] However, in 1913 the states ratified the Sixteenth Amendment to the United States Constitution which provided that:

> The Congress shall have power to lay and collect taxes on incomes, from whatever source derived, without apportionment among the several States, and without regard to any census or enumeration.[415]

This language, while authorizing Congress to apportion the tax on people without regard to census or enumeration, does not negate the language of the Fourteenth Amendment that requires Equal Protection.

Chemerinsky discusses in relation to the dilution of rural voting rights the case of *Lucas v. Forty-Fourth General Assembly*, 377 U.S. 713 (1964), where "the Court said that it was irrelevant that voters, by initiative, had approved the malapportionment (that diluted rural voting power)".[416] Chemerinsky notes that the "Court explained that one-person, one-vote is a Constitutional mandate and that voter

---

framer's intent, with the political process." See, e.g., Robert Bork, *The Tempting of America* 87 (1990).

[414] *Pollock v. Farmers' Loan & Trust Company*, 157 U.S. 429 (1895), *affirmed on rehearing*, 158 U.S. 601 (1895), was a landmark case of the Supreme Court of the United States. In a 5-4 decision, the Supreme Court struck down the income tax imposed because it was not an apportioned direct tax.

[415] U S Const. Amend. 16.

[416] Chemerinsky, 956.

approval does not justify a violation, any more than voter approval would permit the violation of any other constitutional right."[417] As Justice Warren, again writing for the Court about the Equal Protection Clause, contended:

> (a)n individuals constitutionally protected right to cast an equally weighted vote cannot be denied even by a vote of a majority of a State's electorate, if the apportionment scheme adopted by the voters fails to measure up to the requirements of the Equal Protection Clause. Manifestly, the fact that an apportionment plan is adopted in a popular referendum is insufficient to sustain its constitutionality or to induce a court of equity to refuse to act.[418]

This principle is that if the electorate – the people themselves – are unable to transgress or overrule the Equal Protection Clause, then it is axiomatic that a legislature which represents the people is equally unable to overrule the Equal Protection Clause. For this reason, neither the Federal Congress nor State legislatures may overrule the Equal Protection Clause and impose a graduated progressive income tax that clearly discriminates against workers, entrepreneurs, and other workers who earn more than the minimum wage.[419] The Equal Protection Clause should not just benefit the poor and minorities;

---

[417] Chemerinsky, 956.

[418] *Lucas v. Forty-Fourth General Assembly*, 377 U.S. 713,736 (1964).

[419] Many minimum wage earners are in service industries where tips are awarded by customers when they receive exemplary support. The customers do not employ the service workers. The customers have no obligation to register with the government or report the tips to the government. Instead, the customers provide the tips as gifts; and these tips, which are not mandatory but are given in gratitude, should not be taxed as routine income. Nor should exemplary service providers be required, without their consent, to share their gifts with other less productive coworkers.

the Equal Protection Clause must protect all people and should be used to abolish the progressive income tax rates.

The elites use the tax code to deduct the costs of their luxury travel on private jets and relaxing stays in resort hotels by claiming them as business expenses. [420] Nevertheless, the elites try to curry favor with their Veejack faithful supporters through the use of empty slogans like "soak the rich" and "get them to pay their fair share" while using the tax code to trample on the workers and entrepreneurs with progressive tax rates and limited deductions.

The elites want to impose a heavier tax burden on working people than they do on non-working people, and to progressively impose higher tax burdens on people who work more than one job to increase their family's income. A worker who earns a basic union wage in a primary occupation and has outside income from a second job is taxed at a higher rate because the additional income is not taxed at the same rate as the basic union wage. Instead, with the added income generated by industrious hard work in an additional part-time job, the worker's wages are now taxed at a higher rate.

At the same time, the recipients of government charity programs of cash, food, or vouchers are taxed little if at all; and hence these charity recipients have no incentive to elect legislative representatives that promise to keep taxes uniform and reasonable. The reasons the government does not impose an equal tax on benefits to charity recipients is not clear.

It is shocking to realize that the salaries paid to members of the military, who are called upon to risk their lives in dangerous activities and combat are taxed on their income. [421] Thus, military members who may be called to make the ultimate sacrifice are taxed on their meager income. Yet migrants, who enter the United States illegally, are provided free transportation, food debit cards, housing, health coverage, and other benefits and are not taxed on the

---

[420] See, e.g., 26 United States Code §162(a)(2) authorizing deduction of all the ordinary and necessary expenses paid for "traveling expenses."

[421] Internal Revenue Service Publication 3 "Armed Forces Tax Guide".

receipt of these benefits that are the same as income.[422] Government funds paid to members of the civil service,[423] politicians, consultants and others are subject to tax.[424] If the recipients of charity were taxed on their benefits, they would gain an appreciation for why hardworking, citizens resent the income tax. And paying taxes on their government-funded benefits may incentivize charity recipients to obtain work so that they can earn and keep more of their own money.

As the vast majority of recipients of government charity are in urban areas the elites who used *Reynolds* to dominate state governments are able to impose similar progressive tax rate increases for state income taxes. The inequitable application of the Fourteenth Amendment to electorally dominate rural and working people, while at the same time draining their financial resources with increasingly higher tax rates, is just one example of the Veejack religious elites using their political power to discriminate against rural and working people.

Not surprisingly, the progressives encourage discrimination based on wealth to impose higher taxes on working people, entrepreneurs, and small and family-owned businesses. Erwin Chemerinsky, the Dean of the University of California Berkeley School of Law, and famous for his writings on Constitutional law has formulated a concept he describes in his casebook on Constitutional law[425] as "Wealth Discrimination".[426] However, the Wealth Discrimination that Chemerinsky explores is limited to discrimination against the poor. Chemerinsky never addresses the inequity of the income tax that progressively increases as workers hard work results in increased income.

---

[422] The Federal government avoids legislative restrictions on providing benefits to illegal immigrants by funneling Federal grant funds to States, cities, and nonprofit organizations that are not blocked from providing such benefits.

[423] Internal Revenue Code section 3401(c)

[424] 26 U.S.C. §1; 26 U.S.C. §6012; and 26 U.S.C. §6151.

[425] Chemerinsky.

[426] Chemerinsky, 850.

Chemerinsky lists a number of Supreme Court cases that looked to the equal protection clause of the 14th Amendment to prohibit discrimination against low-income earners or no-income people. For example, he points out that the Supreme Court[427] held that "it violated equal protection to deny free trial transcripts to indigent criminal defendants . . .."[428] In that case, the Supreme Court ruled that "a State can no more discriminate on account of poverty than on account of religion, race, or color."[429] In a separate case the Supreme Court observed that "(l)ines drawn on the basis of wealth and property, like those of race, are traditionally disfavored."[430] The standard for determining wealth discrimination, the Supreme Court held, is to use a "rational basis review."[431]

Unfortunately, progressive legislation targeting the rich is intentional discrimination based on wealth; and this intentional discrimination based on wealth deserves a Constitutional challenge to end the practice. The rewards inherent in hard work, intense effort, and scholastic achievement should not result in economic discrimination. Instead, the generation of wealth by workers and entrepreneurs should be treated equally with those who generate less wealth or income. As a caveat, a conscientious society may use tax revenue to ensure that all people lawfully residing in the United States receive enough food, shelter, and medical care to survive.

---

[427] *Griffen v. Illinois*, 351 U.S. 12 (1956).

[428] Chemerinsky, 850.

[429] *Griffen v. Illinois*, 351 U.S. 12, 17 (1956).

[430] *Harper v. Virginia Board of Elections*, 383 U.S. 663, 668 (1966).

[431] Chemerinsky, 850, citing *San Antonio School District v. Rodriquez*, 411 U.S. 1 (1973).

CHAPTER NINE

SYNCRETIC JUDEO-CHRISTIAN CAMOUFLAGE

The Veejack religion has tried to coopt the Old Testament (Tanakh), the Christian gospel, and Jesus's teachings, to convert to the Veejack religion many religious leaders within some Judeo-Christian denominations.[432] The Veejack religion's proselytizing has convinced these leaders to reject the Ten Commandments, reject Jesus's message of love for God and love for each other, and reject the inclusive nature of the Judeo-Christian religions. The Veejack religion has exposed the passionate weakness of many Judeo-Christian theologians. It has led to the moral failures of numerous inhabitants of sacred pulpits. It has instituted a disappointing lack of leadership to address sin within their midst. And instilled a false history of supporting the privileged over the oppressed. This has caused the Judeo-Christian community to stagnate and accept the morally and historically ambiguous falsehoods propagated by the Veejack religion. The most destructive blow to the Judeo-Christian faith and its message is the acceptance by too many rabbis, priests,

---

[432] Sadly, these Judeo-Christian leaders do not recognize that they have been converted and have adopted without question the "truths" of the Veejack religion.

pastors, deacons and lay persons of the theory that the suffering and/ or sins of previous generations of people should be visited on the wrongdoer's direct descendants. And this generationally descending guilt is also visited upon all people, regardless of ancestry, that share the offending wrongdoers' racial, ethnic, sexual, gender, and/or other characteristics.

Prior to the message of love, forgiveness, and charity that the Judeo-Christian religions brought to the world; prior to the message of universal love, redemption, and forgiveness that Jesus learned from studying the Old Testament scriptures; prior to the understanding that God did not favor certain peoples, tribes or groups, but loved all people; prior to these seismic shifts in the perception of God and his message, the people were divided into exclusionary racial, ethnic, tribal and other religious collectives that preyed on each other to the detriment of everybody. The goal of the Veejack religion is to reinstitute division based on race, ethnicity, gender and other irrelevant criteria – rather than recognizing that everyone is a child of God and welcome to receive the love of the Judeo-Christian congregation. Unfortunately, the Judeo-Christian faiths have too readily accepted division along these lines as a theological construct within their faiths. Emphatically, dividing people along artificial lines is not acceptable. It is repugnant to Judeo-Christian beliefs.

All human activity suffers from the possibility that it will be coopted, abused, and misused by wretched, evil, and brutal people. In the past, evil people have been able to temporarily garb Judeo-Christian teachings in the robes of hatred, oppression, and prejudice; but only temporarily. Despite the horrors of the purges of the various early heresies, despite the brutality of the Spanish Inquisition, the cruelty of missionaries to indigenous peoples, support for slavery in the Americas, and despite the rhetoric that tried to cover the genocidal madness of the Nazi exterminations; even these were temporary. Not only were they temporary, but they were ended by other Judeo-Christian people who were appalled, motivated and moved to action by the disgrace inflicted on their faith by those monsters.

The Veejack religion delights in emotionally bombarding people with stories of the suffering of earlier generations. The Veejack religion broadly indicts whole races, ethnic groups, religions, sexes and gender orientations as somehow responsible for the actions of people who lived hundreds of years earlier. The Veejack religion rouses to emotional frenzy people who may, or may not, be the descendants of those who suffered; even when the people aroused to frenzy are generations removed from the suffering. It is wrong, immoral and against Judeo-Christian values to impose, as does the Veejack religion, its theories of ancestral guilt on future generations; and it is equally immoral and destructive to teach people that they have the right to covet the wealth of others and to steal it by any means.

At this point it is important to expose one of the most effective ploys of the Veejack religion to destroy Judeo-Christian beliefs. The ploy is to use syncretic sophistry to mutate the Old Testament (Tanakh) and the gospel of Jesus Christ into a weapon to destroy the Judeo-Christian faith it purports to support. For those unused to theological discourse, the term "syncretism" means the joining together, or amalgamation, of different religions, cultures or ideologies to form a new, different religion.

The Clerics of the Veejack Religion

Most religions have rabbis, ministers, priests, Imams, gurus, or shamans as the spiritual leaders and arbiters of the faith. The Veejack religion is unique because it fails to identify itself as a religion, so its spiritual leaders must adopt public personas in other disciplines. The most popular personas for the Veejack religion's spiritual leaders are politicians; media personalities; broadcast and print commentators; internet influencers; and stage and screen performers. Surprisingly, many of the Veejack religion's spiritual leaders are lay supervisors in Judeo-Christian denominations and may even include ordained ministers, priests, nuns, and rabbis. Veejack religious spiritual leaders also include academic professors teaching theology in religious institutions. Many of the Veejack religion's spiritual leaders, collectively known for the purposes of this essay as "Veejack clerics", may not even recognize the duality of, and contradictions within, their roles.

While some Veejack clerics recognize their masquerade, most seem not to recognize their role as proselytizers and proponents of the Veejack religion's theology. These Veejack clerics have a significant role within the Veejack religion because they maintain the veneer that the Veejack religion does not exist as a separate theological faith. They believe that the Veejack religion is not a thriving faith with its own theology but is merely an ideology within the mainstream of political dialogue. However, the Veejack religion's politicians and media personalities propagate the ever-evolving doctrines and "truths" of the Veejack religion's often internally and theologically contradictory beliefs. Supporting the Veejack clerics are the stage and screen performers who serve as the Veejack religion's cheer leaders and intellectual enforcers.

The Veejack religion does not have identified physical structures for its services; and its services are more often than not virtual, rather than in person. Nevertheless, the Veejack religion does have counterparts to the traditional physical structures used by other religions. The highest level of Veejack religious worship, the equivalent of the Christian Cathedral, Islamic Mosque, or Jewish Temple is cable television. The next level down, the equivalent of the traditional neighborhood church is the internet, from which the Veejack religion's influencers provide guidance and explain the "truths" that are currently in fashion within its elites. Below the internet-church, the equivalent of the small chapel, are the Veejack religion's TV presenters and radio hosts. The radio hosts offer a non-visual, comforting explanation and discussion of the Veejack religion's "truths" and doctrines. The equivalent for the Veejack religion of the sacristy includes written guidance from the elites. Their writings can be digested slowly and contemplated by the literate members of the religion.

A feature common to many religions is the practice of confession.[433] During the practice of confession, a congregant discloses sins to a priest, takes responsibility for them, and seeks penance.[434] The disclosure of sins to an ordained priest, minister, pastor, rabbi, mullah, or other properly cleared church leader are protected from disclosure.[435] And, even if a crime is disclosed the disclosure is privileged and the state may not demand that the information be shared with law enforcement or parties to litigation. This practice is most commonly portrayed in film or television showing the Catholic practice of the penitent member entering a private booth within a church. The confessing penitent enters a booth which is side-by-side with another booth into which the Priest who "hears" the confession enters.[436]

The Veejack religion, which denies its own existence, is unable to ordain its selected elites so that they are authorized and may hear and protect confessional statements. Yet many, if not all, humans need the release that confession and sharing brings. To overcome this hurdle, the Veejack religion welcomed a Supreme Court decision

---

[433] See, e.g., Catechism of the Catholic Church, Section 1457, that reminds "each of the faithful is bound by an obligation faithfully to confess serious sins at least once a year." Available at https://www.vatican.va/archive/ENG0015/__P4D.HTM.

[434] See, e.g., Catechism of the Catholic Church, Sections 1455 and 1456 available at https://www.vatican.va/archive/ENG0015/__P4D.HTM

[435] See, e.g., People v. Phillips, New York Court of General Sessions, June 14, 1813. See, also, Code of Canon Law, Title IV, Canon 965, stating "(a) priest alone is the minister of the sacrament of penance," and Canon 983 §1, stating that "(t)he sacramental seal is inviolable; therefore it is absolutely forbidden for a confessor to betray in any way a penitent in words or in any manner and for any reason." Available at https://www.vatican.va/archive/cod-iuris-canonici/eng/documents/cic_lib4-cann959-997_en.html

[436] See, e.g., episodes of the BBC television show "Father Brown" described at https://en.wikipedia.org/wiki/Father_Brown_(2013_TV_series)

that found a privilege of privacy in confessions made to a licensed psychiatrist, psychologist, or clinical social worker.[437]

The Veejack religion's confessional, unlike its equivalent within the Judeo-Christian faiths, is not private unless as noted above the disclosure is made to a licensed mental health professional. Notwithstanding the protection of disclosures to a licensed mental health professional, at the common level of the Veejack religion its adherents are urged to publicly confess their failures and perceived failures. And many times, the perceived failures are related to the practitioner's having accepted or acting upon the wisdom of Judeo-Christian teachings. At the urging of its leaders, the Veejack religion's confessional requires a public recitation of real or imagined sins that welcomes the humiliation of the confessor. Confession in the Veejack religion is best accomplished orally in public places, on cable and internet broadcasts, and by a recitation of transgressions as articles or letters to the editors of newspapers, magazines, and online publications.

The Judeo-Christian and other faiths believe in prayer.[438] The Judeo-Christian faiths teach that prayer is a dialogue between God and humans.[439] The Veejack religion, as a nontheistic religion, does not endorse the concept of prayer. Within the Veejack religion there

---

[437] *Jaffee v. Redmond*, 518 U.S. 1 (1996), recognized that the federal privilege of protecting confidential disclosures clearly applies to psychiatrists and psychologists, and also extends to confidential communications made to licensed social workers in the course of psychotherapy.

[438] See, e.g., Catechism of the Catholic Church, Part Four "Christian Prayer." The Catholic Church teaches that Christians should read the divine Scriptures and remember that "prayer should accompany the reading of Sacred Scripture, so that a dialogue takes place between God and man. For 'we speak to him when we pray; we listen to him when we read the divine oracles.'" Section 2653, available at https://www.vatican.va/archive/ENG0015/__P9D.HTM

[439] See, e.g., Jewish Prayer – Prayer in Judaism, explaining that "Jewish prayer is G-d's way of telling the Jewish people, "speak to Me and I will listen." Three times a day, Jews pray to G-d, thanking Him, praising Him, and beseeching Him for personal requests." Available at https://www.chabad.org/library/article_cdo/aid/862308/jewish/Prayer.htm

is no higher being, deity, or spirit to whom prayers may be offered for intercession, blessing, or relief from crises. Instead, when hardships, loss, pain, death of a loved one, or personal injury afflicts a believer of the Veejack religion, the equivalent of prayer is to express a burst of rage, seethe with fury, and/or engage in a frenzy of violence. As with the Veejack religion's equivalent of confession, the expression of frenzied rage and/or violence as a substitute of prayer to a divine being, is most often performed in public and directed at an authority figure, or a Judeo-Christian belief, spiritual leader, or representation in art, sculpture, or architecture.

BIBLIOGRAPHY

Books

Bible – New Revised Standard Version Catholic Edition (NRSVCE)

Anthony, David W., *The Horse the Wheel and Language – How Bronze-Age Riders from the Eurasian Steppes shaped the Modern World*, Princeton and Oxford: Princeton University Press, 2007.

"Blom, Phillip, *Nature's Mutiny – How the Little Ice Age of the Long Seventeenth Century Transformed the West and Shaped the Present*, New York: Liveright Publishing Corporation, 2019.

Robert Bork, *The Tempting of America - The Political Seduction of the Law*, New York: Free Press; London: Collier Macmillan, 87 (1990).

Carrasco, David, *Religions in Mesoamerica*, 2nd ed., Long Grove, IL: Waveland Press, Inc., 2014.

Chemerinsky, Erwin, *Constitutional Law – Principles and Policies*, 6th Ed., (New York: Wolters Kluwer), 2019.

Collins, John J., *Introduction to the Hebrew Bible*, 3d Ed., Minneapolis: Fortress Press, 2018.

Dostoyevsky, Fyodor, *The Idiot*, 1918, London: William Heinemann, Moulin Digital Editions, 2023, available at https://ia601600.us.archive.org/35/items/dostoyevsky_fyodor_1821_1881_idiot/dostoyevsky_fyodor_1821_1881_idiot.pdf

Durant, Will, *Our Oriental Heritage*, New York: MJF Books, 1935, renewed 1963.

Fisher, Mary Pat, *Living Religions*, Ninth Edition, Published by Pearson. Copyright © 2014 by Pearson Education, Inc.

Gutierrez, Gustavo, *A Theology of Liberation – 15th Anniversary Edition*, Maryknoll, New York: Orbis Books, 2021.

Hahn, Thich Nhat, *Living Buddha, Living Christ*, New York: Riverhead Books, 2007.

Hamilton, Alexander, Madison, James, Rossiter, Clinton, Jay, John, and Kesler, Charles R., *The Federalist Papers*, New York: Signet Classics, an Imprint of New American Library, a Division of Penguin Group (USA), 2005.

Hawthorne, Nathaniel, *The Scarlet Letter*, 2024 London: Penguin Classics.

Hoffer, Eric, *The True Believer – Thoughts on the Nature of Mass Movements*, New York: Harper Perennial Modern Classics, 2010.

Marx, Karl and Engels, Friedrich, *On Religion*, Mineola, New York: Dover Publications, Inc., 2008.

Orwell, George, *1984*, Istanbul: Books & Coffee Publications, 2021.

Orwell, George, *Animal Farm*, Istanbul/Turkiye: Oteki Adam, 2023.

Quran (Koran)

Renan, Ernest, *History of the People of Israel – Till the Time of King David*, London: Chapman and Hall, Ltd., 1888.

Renan, Ernest, *The History of the Origins of Christianity*, London: Mathieson & Co., 1863-1890.

Taylor, Charles, *A Secular Age*, Cambridge, MA: Belknap Press, 2007.

Tracy, David, *Plurality and Ambiguity*, San Francisco: Harper & Row, 1987.

Articles

Black, Riley, "What Happened in the Seconds, Hours, Weeks After the Dino-Killing Asteroid Hit Earth? – The Cretaceous forecast: Tsunamis, a deadly heat pulse, and massive cooling," August 9, 2016, Smithsonian Magazine at https://www.smithsonianmag.com/science-nature/dinosaur-killing-asteroid-impact-chicxulub-crater-timeline-destruction-180973075/

Boissoneault, Lorraine, "What Really Turned the Sahara Desert From a Green Oasis Into a Wasteland? - 10,000 years ago, this iconic desert was unrecognizable. A new hypothesis suggests that humans may have tipped the balance", March 24, 2017, Smithsonian Magazine at https://www.smithsonianmag.com/science-nature/what-really-turned-sahara-desert-green-oasis-wasteland-180962668/

Freeman III, George C., "The Misguided Search for the Constitutional Definition of 'Religion'," 71 Geo. L.J. 1519, 1548 (1983).

Greenberg, David F. and Bystryn, Marcia H., "Christian Intolerance of Homosexuality", *American Journal of Sociology*, 88, No. 3 (1982), pp. 515-548, 530.

Newman, Barbara, "Hildegard of Bingen and the 'Birth of Purgatory'," *Mystics Quarterly*, 19 No. 3, 1993, 90-97, 93.

Harper, Kyle, (from Aeon) "How Climate Change and Plague Helped Bring Down the Roman Empire – We can learn crucial lessons by examining the natural forces that shaped Rome's rise and fall", December 19, 2017, Smithsonian Magazine at https://www.smithsonianmag.com/science-nature/how-climate-change-and-disease-helped-fall-rome-180967591/

Schneiders, Sandra Marie, "Religion vs. Spirituality: A Contemporary Conundrum", *Spiritus: A Journal of Christian Spirituality*, Vol 3, No 2, Fall 2003, 163-185.

Schwarz, Alan, "No Imposition of Religion: The Establishment Clause Value", 77 Yale L.J. 692, 693 (1968).

Stamps, Robert F. (2022) "Christians Must Reach Out to the Oppressed," Say Something Theological: The Student Journal of Theological Studies: Vol. 5: Iss. 1, Article 10; available at https://digitalcommons.lmu.edu/cgi/viewcontent.cgi?article=1061&context=saysomethingtheological

Wright, David K., "Humans as Agents in the Termination of the African Humid Period," January 26, 2017, Frontiers, in Earth Science, 1-14

Religious Organization Documents

Catechism of the Catholic Church, Sections 1455 and 1456 at https:// www.vatican.va/archive/ENG0015/__P4D.HTM

Catechism of the Catholic Church, Section 1457, at https://www. vatican.va/archive/ENG0015/__P4D.HTM.

Catechism of the Catholic Church, at 2270, 2271, 2272, and 2274; available at https://www.vatican.va/archive/ENG0015/_ INDEX.HTM

Catechism of the Catholic Church, Part Four "Christian Prayer," Section 2653, at https://www.vatican.va/archive/ENG0015/__ P9D.HTM

Code of Canon Law, Title IV, Canon 965, at https://www.vatican.va/ archive/cod-iuris-canonici/eng/documents/cic_lib4-cann959-997_ en.html

Declaration of the Dicastery for the Doctrine of the Faith "Dignitas Infinita" on Human Dignity, 08.04.2024 at https://press.vatican.va/ content/salastampa/en/bollettino/pubblico/2024/04/08/240408c. html.

Declaration "Dignitas Infinite" On Human Dignity, Dicastery for the Doctrine of the Faith, April 8, 2024.

Causae et Curae, found at http://home.kpn.nl/i.w.c.emmens/pdf/ causcur.pdf.

Declaration on the Relation of the Church to Non-Christian Religions Nostra Aetate Proclaimed by His Holiness Pope Paul VI, on October 28, 1965.

United Methodist Church's *Social Principles* at https://www.umc. org/en/content/ask-the-umc-what-is-the-united-methodist-position-on-abortion

Social Principles: The Nurturing Community - The Book of Discipline of The United Methodist Church – 2016, at https://www.umc.org/ en/content/social-principles-the-nurturing-community#abortion

Jewish Prayer – Prayer in Judaism, at https://www.chabad.org/library/ article_cdo/aid/862308/jewish/Prayer.htm

Web Sites

Associated Press, "Minnesota governor signs broad abortion rights bill into law", January 31, 2023, and Mekelburg, Madlin, "Do Democrats support abortion up until (and after) birth?", February 27, 2020, PolitiFact at https://www.politifact.com/factchecks/2020/feb/27/ ted-cruz/do-democrats-support-abortion-until-and-after-birt/

"Bay Area Christians fighting city which took down cross: 'They really hate what it stands for' – The cross on Albany Hill had stood for 52 years overlooking the East shore of San Francisco Bay," August 2, 2023 at https://www.foxnews.com/media/bay-area-christians-fighting-city-took-down-cross-really-hate-what-stands-for

Allen, Mercedes, "Trans History 101: Transgender Expression in Ancient Times", February 24, 2016 available at https://www.lgbtqnation.com /2016/02/trans-history-101-transgender-expression-in-ancient-times/

Armstrong, Edward, "The Sahara Desert used to be a green savannah – new research explains why," December 15, 2023, The Conversation at https://theconversation.com/the-sahara-desert-used-to-be-a-green-savannah-new-research-explains-why-216555, published in *Nature Communications*

Andrews, Evan, "8 Reasons It Wasn't Easy Being Spartan - From fitness tests for infants to state-sponsored hazing, find out why these ancient Greek warriors had a rough go of it", at https://www.history.com/news/8-reasons-it-wasnt-easy-being-spartan

Arnall, Alex, "The Maldives is threatened by rising seas – but coastal development is causing even more pressing environmental issues", October 27, 2021, The Conversation at https://theconversation.com/the-maldives-is-threatened-by-rising-seas-but-coastal-development-is-causing-even-more-pressing-environmental-issues-170144.

Besl, J., "The Ever-Shifting—Not Necessarily Shrinking—Pacific Island Nations", September 22, 2021, Hakai Magazine at https://hakaimagazine.com/news/the-ever-shifting-not-necessarily-shrinking-pacific-island-nations/

Chapman, Fern Schumer, "How Religious Shunning Ruins Lives – A form of institutionalized estrangement, shunning hurts health of the excluded", March 27, 2024, *Psychology Today*, at https://www.psychologytoday.com/us/blog/brothers-sisters-strangers/202403/how-religious-shunning-ruins-lives

Dale, Daniel, "Fact check: Biden again falsely claims inflation was 9% when he became president", May 14, 2024, CNN Facts First at https://www.cnn.com/2024/05/14/politics/fact-check-biden-inflation-when-he-became-president?cid=ios_app

Dorgan, Michael, "Catholic monk comes out as transgender with diocese's permission", May 23, 2024, Fox News at https://www.foxnews.com/us/catholic-monk-comes-out-transgender-diocese-permission

Faa, Marian, "Hundreds of Pacific Islands are getting bigger despite global warming", January 7, 2021, News – Pacific Beat at https://www.abc.net.au/news/2021-01-08/why-are-hundreds-of-pacific-islands-getting-bigger/13038430

Fitzpatric, Cara, "The Charter-School Movement's New Divide – A Catholic charter in Oklahoma would represent a profound shift for American education—and for the charter-school movement itself," September 13, 2023, *The Atlantic*, at https://www.theatlantic.com/ideas/archive/2023/09/charter-schools-religion-public-secular/675293/

Gerretsen, Isabelle; Henriques, Martha; Bourke, India; and Sherriff, Lucy, "Exploding craters and overflowing landfills are unexpected sources of methane," April 3, 2024 at https://www.bbc.com/future/article/20240402-the-surprising-sources-of-methane

Glicksman, Eve, "Transgender Today - Throughout history, transgender people have been misunderstood and seldom studied. That's beginning to change," Vol 44, No. 4, April 2013, at https://www.apa.org/monitor/2013/04/transgender

Hagstrom, Anders, "Catholic voters respond after 'devout' Biden once again sides against his Church," April 11, 2024 at https://www.foxnews.com/politics/catholic-voters-respond-devout-biden-once-sides-his-church

Halon, Yael, "DC archbishop jabs Biden as 'cafeteria Catholic' who 'picks and chooses' for his 'political advantage' – Biden has repeatedly described himself as a 'devout Catholic' who attends church regularly," April 1, 2024 at https://www.foxnews.com/media/dc-archbishop-jabs-biden-cafeteria-catholic-who-picks-chooses-political-advantage

Hays, Gabriel, "U.S. Senate candidate goes viral for blaming NY earthquake on climate change, deletes post – Congressman Dan Crenshaw, R-Texas, marveled, 'I was just joking about people blaming climate change and then this genius pops up'," April 6, 2024 at https://www.foxnews.com/media/u-s-senate-candidate-viral-blaming-ny-earthquake-climate-change-deletes-post

Heaton, Thomas (Grantee), "'Ticking Ecological Time Bombs': Thousands of Sunken WWII Ships Rusting at Bottom of Pacific", Pulitzer Center, December 6, 2022, at https://pulitzercenter.org/stories/ticking-ecological-time-bombs-thousands-sunken-wwii-ships-rusting-bottom-pacific

Hernandez, Samantha, "Investigating How Politics Is Affecting Education? Here's What to Know," September 13, 2022, at https://ewa.org/news-explainers/how-politics-affects-education

Hewitt, Hugh, "Morning Glory: the border and 'Catholic social teaching' – If leftists tell you "Catholic social teaching" means an open border, they are either ignorant or lying," March 12, 2024 at https://www.foxnews.com/opinion/morning-glory-border-catholic-social-teaching

Hirst, K. Kris, "What Did Cicero Mean by the Sword of Damocles? - A Roman Moral Philosophy on How to Be Happy", ThoughtCo, April 12, 2018, at https://www.thoughtco.com/what-is-the-sword-of-damocles-117738

Hunter, Heather, "Sunny Hostin speculates cicadas, solar eclipse, and earthquake could be caused by 'climate change'," April 9, 2024 at https://www.msn.com/en-us/tv/news/sunny-hostin-speculates-cicadas-solar-eclipse-and-earthquake-could-be-caused-by-climate-change/ar-BB1lhyje

Lamche, Anna, "China changed village names 'to erase Uyghur culture'", June 20, 2024, BBC at https://www.bbc.com/news/articles/cxrrkl6ve39o

Lim, Clarissa-Jan, "NYPD Storms Columbia University, clears protesters from occupied building," May 1, 2024, MSNBC at https://www.msnbc.com/top-stories/latest/nypd-columbia-ccny-pro-palestinian-protests-arrests-rcna150185

Lindsay, "Brooklyn classroom displays Qatar-funded map where Israel is replaced with Palestine: report", January 12, 2024 at https://www.foxnews.com/media/brooklyn-classroom-displays-qatar-funded-map-where-israel-replaced-palestine-report

Mark, Joshua J., LGBTQ+ in the Ancient World, June 25, 2021 available at Https://www.worldhistory.org/article/1790/lgbtq-in-the-ancient-world/

Moore, Stephen, "The biggest corporate welfare scam ever is green – Never forget, a lot of people are getting really, really rich off climate change hysteria and President Biden is helping them do it," April 10, 2024 at https://www.foxnews.com/opinion/biggest-corporate-welfare-scam-green

Morris, Kyle, "Pelosi rebuked to her face during Oxford debate after condemning Americans clouded by 'guns, gays, God' – Pelosi suggested Americans refuse to listen to Democrats about certain issues due to their beliefs about 'guns, gays, [and] God'", May 11, 2024, Fox News at https://www.foxnews.com/politics/pelosi-rebuked-oxford-debate-condemning-americans-clouded-guns-gays-god

Nelson, Joseph Q., "Washington teacher says schools must do more to keep students' info secret from 'Christo-fascist' parents," February

25, 2023, https://www.foxnews.com/media/washington-teacher-says-schools-keep-students-info-secret-christo-fascist-parents.

Nerozzi, Timothy, "Biden 'doesn't understand the Catholic faith,' bishop says: 'I'm not angry at him, he's just stupid'," April 20, 2024, at https://www.foxnews.com/faith-values/biden-doesnt-understand-catholic-faith-bishop-not-angry-him-hes-just-stupid

Nihlean, Joel, "Can You Truly Be Christian Without Being Some Kind of Socialist? – Christianity and socialism share many overarching goals. When you look at these similarities, making the case the Christians ought to be socialists becomes pretty simple," June 22, 2021, at https://aninjusticemag.com/how-christianity-and-socialism-make-each-other-better-b988dd750fc6.

Powell, Alvin, September 28, 2000, "Fight over Huck Finn continues: Ed School professor wages battle for Twain classic", The Harvard Gazette at https://news.harvard.edu/gazette/story/2000/09/fight-over-huck-finn-continues-ed-school-professor-wages-battle-for-twain-classic/

Rhoden, Giselle and Paul, Dalila, "73 Confederate monuments were removed or renamed last year, report finds", February 3, 2022, CNN at https://www.cnn.com/2022/02/02/us/confederate-monuments-removed-2021-whose-heritage/index.html

Rosch, Carla, "The bloody turtle video that sparked a plastic straw revolution," April 9, 2024 at https://www.bbc.co.uk/future/article/20240402-the-turtle-video-that-sparked-a-plastic-straw-revolution

Ryan, Craig, "Truk Lagoon – The Biggest Graveyard Of Ships In The World", December 1, 2023, NavalHistoria, at https://navalhistoria.com/truk-lagoon/

Ryan, Craig, "USS Oriskany – The Aircraft Carrier that Became an Artificial Reef", October 3, 2023, NavalHistoria, at https://navalhistoria.com/uss-oriskany/

Ryan, Craig, "SS Thistlegorm – A Divers Paradise", September 26, 2023, NavalHistoria, at https://navalhistoria.com/ss-thistlegorm/#google_vignette

Sawchuck, Stephen, "Are Teachers Obliged to Tell Parents Their Child Might Be Trans? Courts May Soon Decide," April 28, 2022, available at https://www.edweek.org/policy-politics/are-teachers-obliged-to-tell-parents-their-child-might-be-trans-courts-may-soon-decide/2022/04.

Shaw, Adam, "San Francisco archbishop bars Pelosi from receiving Holy Communion due to abortion support – Pelosi has said she is a 'devout' Catholic despite her abortion advocacy," May 20, 2022, at https://www.foxnews.com/politics/san-francisco-archbishop-pelosi-communion-abortion-support

Simon, James and Merrill, Bruce, "Political socialization in the classroom revisited: the Kids Voting program," *The Social Science Journal* v. 35 no1 (1998) p. 29-42, discussed at https://www2.lewisu.edu/~gazianjo/political_socialization_in_the_c.htm

Sword, Rosemary K.M., and Zimbardo, Phillip, "Shunning: The Ultimate Rejection – What does it mean when we shun others or are shunned?", February 1, 2013, *Psychology Today*, at https://www.psychologytoday.com/us/blog/the-time-cure/201302/shunning-the-ultimate-rejection

Tietz, Kendall, "Religious-themed designs banned from White House Easter egg art contest," March 29, 2024, at https://www.

foxnews.com/media/religious-themed-designs-banned-white-house-easter-egg-art-contest

Walker, Tim, "'Education is Political': Neutrality in the Classroom Shortchanges Students – Discussing human rights and equity should be welcomed in classrooms, not dismissed as 'partisanship' or 'politics'", December 11, 2018, at https://www.nea.org/nea-today/all-news-articles/education-political-neutrality-classroom-shortchanges-student

Wulfsohn, Joseph A., "NBC's Ronna McDaniel meltdown: Falsehoods and debunked narratives MSNBC promoted on its 'sacred airwaves'", March 30, 2024 at https://www.foxnews.com/media/nbcs-ronna-mcdaniel-meltdown-falsehoods-debunked-narratives-msnbc-promoted-sacred-airwaves

Yousef, Odette and Hagen, Lisa, "Unpacking the truth of antisemitism on college campuses" April 25, 2024, NPR, at https://www.npr.org/2024/04/25/1247253244/unpacking-the-truth-of-antisemitism-on-college-campuses

Zengarini, Lisa, "Pope Francis: Gender ideology is the ugliest danger of our time," Vatican News at https://www.vaticannews.va/en/pope/news/2024-03/pope-francis-gender-ideology-is-the-ugliest-danger-of-our-time.html.

Zhong, Raymond and Gulley, Jason "The Vanishing Islands that Failed to Vanish", June 26, 2024, New York Times at https://www.nytimes.com/2024/06/27/briefing/maldives-atolls-climate-change.html

Zummo, Lynne, "Stanford education scholar explores how political views influence teens' understanding of climate change," April 21, 2020, at https://ed.stanford.edu/news/stanford-education-scholar-explores-how-political-views-influence-teens-understanding-climate

"An Additional 1000 ft of RVs and Encampments Cleared at Ballona Wetlands", August 2, 2023, Westside Current at https://www.westsidecurrent.com/news/an-additional-1000-ft-of-rvs-and-encampments-cleared-at-ballona-wetlands/article_50de97cc-2cb4-11ee-8e94-4b430d1247d0.html

"Bay Area Christians fighting city which took down cross: 'They really hate what it stands for' – The cross on Albany Hill had stood for 52 years overlooking the East shore of San Francisco Bay," August 2, 2023 at https://www.foxnews.com/media/bay-area-christians-fighting-city-took-down-cross-really-hate-what-stands-for

"Mental Health Challenges of Young Adults Illuminated in New Report – Making Caring Common identifies several drivers of young adults' emotional challenges, including a lack of meaning and purpose," October 24, 2023, posted by News Editor, Harvard Graduate School of Education at https://www.gse.harvard.edu/ideas/news/23/10/mental-health-challenges-young-adults-illuminated-new-report

"The Law: The Court's Uncompromising Libertarian". Time.com. November 24, 1975 at https://time.com/archive/6847475/the-law-the-courts-uncompromising-libertarian/

"RV encampment impacting the Ballona Freshwater Marsh", January 16, 2022, Spectrum News at https://spectrumnews1.com/ca/la-west/homelessness/2022/01/16/rv-encampment-is-impacting-the-ballona-freshwater-marsh

https://www.bing.com/videos/search?q=byrids%20pretty%20boy%20flloyd%20videos&FORM=VIRE0&mid=B672B75F5FC

C6C967997B672B75F5FCC6C967997&view=detail&ru=%2F
search%3Fq%3Dbyrids%20pretty%20boy%20flloyd.

https://www.britannica.com/science/intertropical-convergence-zone

https://education.nationalgeographic.org/resource/earth-day/

https://www2.classics.upenn.edu/myth/php/homer/index.
php?page=gods

https://en.wikipedia.org/wiki/Cafeteria_Catholicism

https://en.wikipedia.org/wiki/Cancel_culture

https://en.wikipedia.org/wiki/Classical_element

https://en.wikipedia.org/wiki/Deva_(Hinduism)

https://en.wikipedia.org/wiki/Dharma

https://en.wikipedia.org/wiki/Ebonics_(word)

https://en.wikipedia.org/wiki/Father_Brown_(2013_TV_series)

https://en.wikipedia.org/wiki/Festivus

https://en.wikipedia.org/wiki/Ficus_religiosa

https://en.wikipedia.org/wiki/Gender_fluidity

https://en.wikipedia.org/wiki/Interglacial

https://en.wikipedia.org/wiki/Karma

https://en.wikipedia.org/wiki/%C4%80tman_(Hinduism)

https://en.wikipedia.org/wiki/Last_Glacial_Period

https://en.wikipedia.org/wiki/Little_Ice_Age

https://en.wikipedia.org/wiki/Medieval_Warm_Period

https://en.wikipedia.org/wiki/Milankovitch_cycles

https://en.wikipedia.org/wiki/Milutin_Milankovic

https://en.wikipedia.org/wiki/Mother_goddess

https://en.wikipedia.org/wiki/Passover

https://en.wikipedia.org/wiki/Quran

https://en.wikipedia.org/wiki/Shakti

https://en.wikipedia.org/wiki/Situational_ethics

https://en.wikipedia.org/wiki/Wicca

https://en.wikipedia.org/wiki/African-American_Vernacular_English_and_social_context#Oakland_Ebonics_resolution

https://en.wikipedia.org/wiki/Weather_god

https://en.wikipedia.org/wiki/The_Western_Journal

https://en.wikipedia.org/wiki/Youngest_Toba_eruption

https://www.earthday.org/wp-content/uploads/2024/04/Climate-Education-vs-The-Climate-Crisis.pdf

https://earthobservatory.nasa.gov/world-of-change/global-temperatures

https://www.britannica.com/biography/Hugo-Grotius

https://www.britannica.com/science/intertropical-convergence-zone

https://www.britannica.com/topic/Passover

https://libquotes.com/ernest-renan/quote/lbr9i4x

https://stormguardrc.com/the-history-of-weather-gods/

https://www.westernjournal.com/study-nearly-2-dozen-scientists-finds-sun-not-co2-may-chief-cause-global-warming/

"New research reveals why and when the Sahara Desert was green," University of Bristol, December 13, 2023, at https://phys.org/news/2023-09-reveals-sahara-green.html#:~:text=Lead%20author%20Dr.%20Edward%20Armstrong%2C%20a%20climate%20scientist,the%20most%20remarkable%20environmental%20changes%20on%20the%20planet.%22

https://wiccaliving.com/essentials-wicca/

https://www.nasa.gov/centers-and-facilities/goddard/nasa-satellite-reveals-how-much-saharan-dust-feeds-amazons-plants/

https://www.youtube.com/watch?v=l-JW4DKxwQM

Human Events Staff, "Study Finds Sun May Be Leading Cause of Global Warming," August 26, 2021, at https://humanevents.com/2021/08/26/study-finds-sun-may-be-leading-cause-of-global-warming/

United States Documents

United States Constitution
    Amendment 1
    Amendment 14
    Amendment 16, §1
    Art 1, §2
    Art. 1, §3, cl. 1, amended 1919 (U.S. Const. Amend. XVII)

H.R.1308 – *Religious Freedom Restoration Act of 1993*, enacted as Public Law No.: 103-141, and codified at 42 U.S.C. § 2000bb et seq.

"Judicial Procedures Reform Bill of 1937" at https://en.wikipedia.org/wiki/Judicial_Procedures_Reform_Bill_of_1937

26 United States Code §1;

26 United States Code §162(a)(2)

26 United States Code §6012

26 United States Code §6151

Internal Revenue Service Publication 3 "Armed Forces Tax Guide"

Internal Revenue Code section 3401(c)

Abington School District. V. Schempp, 374 U.S. 203 (1963)

Baker v. Carr, 369 U.S. 186 (1962)

Ball v. James, 451 U.S. 355 (1981)

Board of Estimates v. Morris, 489 U.S. 688 (1989

Cantwell v. Connecticut, 310 U.S. 296 (1940)

Capitol Square Review and Advisory Board v. Pinette, 515 U.S. 753 (1995)

Colegrove v. Green, 328 U.S. 549 (1946

County of Allegheny v. American Civil Liberties Union, Greater Pittsburgh Chapter, 492 U.S. 573, 627 (1989)

Everson v. Board of Education, 330 U.S. 1 (1947)

Gray v. Sanders, 372 U.S. 368 (1963)

Griffen v. Illinois, 351 U.S. 12 (1956)

Harper v. Virginia Board of Elections, 383 U.S. 663, 668 (1966)

Jacobellis v. Ohio, 378 U.S. 184 (1964)

Jaffee v. Redmond, 518 U.S. 1 (1996)

Lee v. Weisman, 505 U.S. 577 (1992)

Lucas v. Forty-Fourth General Assembly, 377 U.S. 713 (1964)

Malnak v. Yogi, 440 F. Supp. 1284 (D.N.J. 1977)

Marsh v. Chamber, 463 U.S. 783 (1983)

Pollock v. Farmers' Loan & Trust Company, 157 U.S. 429 (1895), *affirmed on rehearing*, 158 U.S. 601 (1895)

Reynolds v. Sims, 377 U.S. 533 (1964)

San Antonio School District v. Rodriquez, 411 U.S. 1 (1973)

Torcaso v. Watkins, 367 U.S. 488, 495 (1961)

Thomas v. Review Bd., Ind. Empl. Sec. Div., 450 U.S. 707, 714 (1981)

People v. Phillips, New York Court of General Sessions, June 14, 1813

International Documents

1987 Montreal Protocol on Substances that Deplete the Ozone Layer, 1522 UNTS 3, 26 ILM 1541, 1550 (1987).

International Energy Agency (December 2023) at https://www.iea.org/data-and-statistics/charts/global-coal-consumption-2020-2023

https://www.iea.org/reports/coal-2023/demand

https://www.iea.org/reports/coal-2023